Born near Nizhni Novgorod in 1906, ELENA
SKRJABINA grew up in St. Petersburg, now Leningrad, where her father was a member of the last
Russian parliament before the Revolution. When
the Germans attacked in 1941, she was pursuing
graduate studies in French literature and was married to engineer Sergei Skrjabin, with whom she
had two children. In 1950 Elena Skrjabina came to
the United States. She earned a doctorate in French
and comparative literature from Syracuse University, and since 1960 has been Professor of Russian at the University of Iowa.

NORMAN LUXENBURG, the editor and translator, is
Professor of Russian at the University of Iowa.

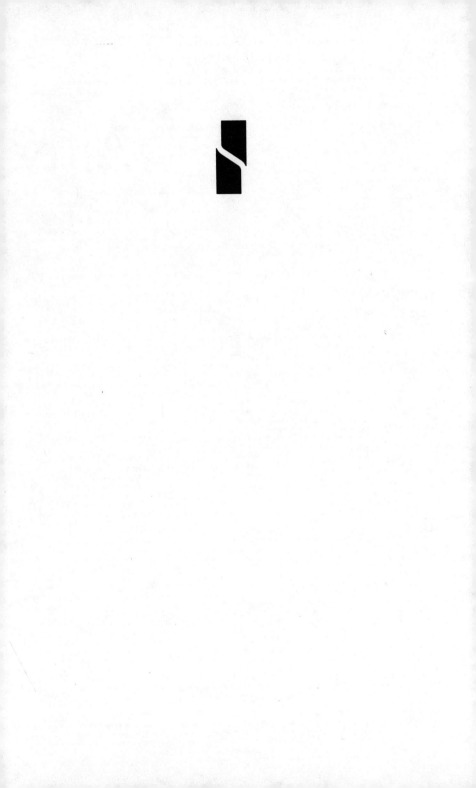

After

From

A Diary

Leningrad

the Caucasus to the Rhine

AUGUST 9, 1942–MARCH 25, 1945

of Survival During World War II

by

ELENA SKRJABINA

Translated, Edited, and with an Introduction by NORMAN LUXENBURG

Southern Illinois University Press

Carbondale and Edwardsville

Feffer & Simons, Inc., *London and Amsterdam*

Library of Congress Cataloging in Publication Data

Skrjabina, Elena
    After Leningrad.

    First pt. of this diary, previously published in Russian, was combined with a later account and published in German in 1972 under title: Leningrader Tagebuch.
    Includes index.
    1. World War, 1939–1945—Personal narratives, Russian. 2. Skrjabina, Elena. 3. Refugees—Russia—Biography. 4. World War, 1939–1945—Russia. 5. Russia—History—German occupation, 1941–1944. I. Luxenburg, Norman, 1927–   II. Title.
D811.5.S35413   940.54'82'47   78–18872
ISBN 0–8093–0856–8

Printed by offset lithography in the United States of America
Designed by Janet Anderson

CONTENTS

ILLUSTRATIONS AND MAPS

ILLUSTRATIONS

MAPS

INTRODUCTION

I first became acquainted with Elena Skrjabina in 1963 at a Modern Language Conference in Minneapolis where she delivered a paper on the Russian social humorist Mikhail Zoshenko (Zoschenko). I enjoyed her talk and spoke with her about it. Thus when subsequently a colleague informed me that her diary of the siege of Leningrad had been published in Russian, I was interested in seeing it, intending more or less to get a general idea of its contents rather than actually reading it thoroughly. As I skimmed through the first few pages, however, my attention was drawn to such a degree that I had to read it to the end before I could put it down.

In 1967 I moved to the University of Iowa, becoming chairman of the Russian department in which Elena Skrjabina was a professor. Since her book, *Les Faux Dieux*, had recently appeared and since Southern Illinois University Press was preparing to publish her *Siege and Survival*, she was receptive to suggestions that she continue her fascinating writing about the tremendously important events to which she had been an eyewitness. Accordingly, she arranged her diary of the happenings from the coming of the Germans into the Caucasus in 1942 to the arrival of the Americans in the Rhineland in 1945. This account, together with the previous part, was published in 1972 under the title *Leningrader Tagebuch* by the Biederstein Verlag.

For some reason it was not until 1977 that either Professor Skrjabina or I thought seriously about translating this account into English. In the meantime Professor Skrjabina has recently completed her extremely interesting account, "Coming of Age in Revolution, Civil War, and Terror." My translation of that work is now virtually ready.

To set the present diary account in historical perspective,

however, we must go back to the time just preceding World War II. In late August, 1939, as war clouds were darkening over Europe, the world was astounded by the news that the Soviet Union and Hitlerite Germany had signed a nonaggression pact. This was all the more remarkable since throughout the 1930s none had railed more against the Bolshevik menace than had the Nazis; similarly, none had been more savage in their denunciation of the Nazi beasts than had the Soviets. Thus this Nazi–Soviet accord took the diplomatic world by surprise.

Hitler, now assured of Russian neutrality, felt free to press his claims against Poland despite Anglo–French insistence that they would support Poland if the latter were attacked. The new German Siegfried Line in the West could keep the French and British at bay while he finished with the Poles, and in the event of a somewhat protracted war, he could count on Russian supplies to avoid the worst stringencies of an Allied blockade. On September 1, 1939, Nazi forces swarmed into Poland. After seventeen days of fighting, the Poles were smashed and reeling. However, units were retreating to the east hoping to make a stand deeper in Poland. There the Germans would have to fight in worse terrain under worsening weather conditions, with more extended communication lines, while the Poles hoped to be supplied through Rumania. All the time, Britain would be strengthening her forces on Germany's Western Front. While it is doubtful that the Poles could have held out even in the east, the sudden invasion of Poland by the Russians on September 17 made further resistance virtually impossible. The Soviets and Germans shortly thereafter concluded a treaty of friendship and established a demarcation line between them; as a result of this and other agreements, the Soviets agreed to supply Germany with many of the raw materials necessary to carry on war.

In the spring of 1940, Nazi forces overran Denmark and Norway. In May they struck in the West. Holland fell in less than a week, Belgium in less than three, and even France, believed by many to have had the finest army in the world, fell within six weeks. Most of the British expeditionary forces fighting with the French had been able to get back to England; however, they had been forced to abandon virtually all their military equipment. Germany was thus master of the European mainland from the Russian Border to the English channel.

Of the three southern peninsulas of Europe, the Italian under Benito Mussolini was already in the war on Hitler's side. The Iberian was under the control of Francisco Franco, who was indebted to Mussolini and Hitler for aid he had received in the Spanish Civil War, and the Balkan seemed to be becoming drawn into the Nazi orbit as German influence, already paramount in Hungary, became more and more predominant in Rumania and Bulgaria.

Stalin, extremely worried by the tremendous German successes, feverishly tried to increase Russian military strength while at the same time doing everything possible not to offend Hitler. He had already taken advantage of German preoccupation in the West in June of 1940 to annex the Baltic republics of Latvia, Estonia, and Lithuania, and shortly thereafter he had forced Rumania to cede to him the province of Bessarabia and part of Bukovina, territories containing some four million persons. Rumania, which had thereby already lost four million of her population of seventeen million to the USSR, now found herself faced with further demands by her neighbors. Under these conditions, Rumania announced that she had freely entered the sphere of the Axis (Nazi-Italian) powers and in October 1940, some German forces entered Rumania in order, as they told the Soviets, "to protect the oil fields." Regardless of how the Germans attempted to explain the presence of German troops in Rumania, the Soviets felt uneasy.

Meanwhile Hitler stood at the crossroads. He had been unable to wrest from the British uncontested air supremacy over the channel and the English coast. It was possible to attempt a cross-channel invasion without having uncontrolled air superiority. However, before such enormous risks, Hitler hesitated. What might happen if he should become bogged down in an English campaign and if the Russians would hold up supplies or, even worse, attack? He himself had invoked the law of the jungle and the Soviets in their attack on Finland in the winter of 1939–40 had shown themselves bound by no moral scruples. Perhaps he could get the Russians to join him against the British if enough prospective booty were held out to them in the Middle East and India.

It was against this background, therefore, that Russian Foreign Minister Molotov arrived in Berlin for talks in November 1940. Here the Germans tried to interest the Soviets in striking at the British lifeline in the Middle East. Molotov was more interested in gaining a predominant role for Russia in Rumania and the Balkans. The talks thus ended in failure and Hitler gave orders to continue drawing up plans for "Operation Barbarossa," the invasion of Russia, which was intended to begin in May 1941.

Hitler's decision was hastened by the knowledge that England's overseas dominions were sending more and more men and material to aid her. The United States was also beginning to send aid to England. Time, therefore, was not fighting for Germany. If he could gain a quick victory over Russia and avail himself of the latter's enormous raw materials, he would then be in an invincible position either to continue the war or to make peace on his terms.

Throughout the winter and spring of 1941, the Soviet leaders continued to fulfill all their trade and treaty obligations toward Germany. Hostile comment toward the latter not only did not appear in the Soviet press, but was kept out of the foreign

Communist press, which continued to denounce World War II as an imperialist, capitalist war, and blame Britain for its continuance.

Meanwhile, Hitler's inept ally, Mussolini, had become bogged down in a campaign against Greece which he, disappointed with the meager gains Italy had so far acquired, and seeking military glory, had begun in October 1940. Hitler, unwilling to risk an invasion of Russia when his southern flank might be exposed to British planes and forces operating out of Greece, decided on a lightning campaign in the Balkans in April 1941. Because of this campaign, it was not until late June, rather than May, that his forces were in position for an attack on the Soviet Union.

Warnings that the Germans were preparing to attack had come to the Soviet leader from a number of sources, including even Winston Churchill. Stalin had dismissed these warnings as provocations; however, he was worried and did greatly strengthen Soviet forces in the front areas and did everything possible to keep from provoking a German attack.

The German attack, coming as it did on June 21, 1941, apparently caught the Soviet leaders by complete surprise. The Russian civilian population, while it had always felt that there was something unnatural about the friendship pact with Germany, had absolutely no inkling that war was imminent. The reactions of quite a significant cross section of Russians are brought out in this diary.

In the opening stages of the war the Germans advanced with great speed, Army Group North heading for Leningrad something like five hundred miles from the German-Soviet border, while the other two army groups headed for Moscow and the Ukraine respectively. During these opening battles Russian resistance was spotty, extremely stubborn resistance by some units, lack of will to fight by others. Within two days, Vilna had fallen; within two weeks, Riga. More than six hundred thousand Russian prisoners were taken in the encirclement at Bialystok near the frontier; about the same number were taken in the battle of Vyazma, and again as many in the battle for Kiev, which the Germans took on September 19, 1941. Elena Skrjabina's diary, *Siege and Survival* (Southern Illinois University Press, 1971), provides a strong insight into the type of spirit prevailing among many Russians in Leningrad at that time. In certain areas of White Russia and the Ukraine, the Germans were even greeted as liberators by significant segments of the population, for they had suffered grievously under the Stalinization of the preceding years. There were many Russians who did not care to fight for Stalin and the type of Communism they had experienced.

However, Hitler was revealing that he had no intention of confining this operation to a battle to bring down Communism. This was being turned into a battle against the Slavs, for living room in the East and huge estates to reward certain Nazi paladins. The Nazi leader, drunk with previous successes, felt no necessity to honor the normal rules of warfare and word of Nazi excesses drifted back to the Russians. But meanwhile the Russians were rallying. Stalin's appeal to Russian national feeling was bearing fruit, and the Nazi advance on the Leningrad and Moscow fronts was slowed down considerably in the fall of 1941, as Leningrad, now cut off from the rest of the country, entered its period of martyrdom. Those women, children, and other dependents who had not already abandoned the city before the Germans cut the roads began to starve. German offensive operations were halted and the Russians began a number of small counter attacks. Lake Ladoga froze and a very tenuous evacuation and supply route across the frozen lake was opened up. It was across this lake that Elena Skrjabina and thousands of emaciated Leningraders were evacuated during that first horrible winter of war.

With the end of winter and the advent of better weather the Germans in 1942 began a new push into southern Russia; one army swept to the Volga at Stalingrad, while other forces moved into the Caucasus. On August 9, 1942, German tanks swept deep into the Caucasus, occupying the resort city of Pyatigorsk where Elena Skrjabina, then a young mother of two boys, was living. The previous winter, that of 1941–42, she had undergone all the horrors and tragedies of the siege of Leningrad. These she had recounted quite simply and dramatically in her diary *Siege and Survival*. This diary remains a testimonial, a day-by-day description of the greatest, and because of its immense scope, the most horrible siege in world history. Perhaps one million persons died of hunger and its effects during this period.

For Elena Skrjabina, then finishing her long-interrupted advanced studies in French at the Leningrad Institute of Foreign Languages, the question of evacuation was one of survival for herself and her family. In the spring of 1942, she and her two sons, Yuri aged five, and Dima aged fourteen, succeeded in reaching Pyatigorsk, having survived the perilous and arduous evacuation from Leningrad only with the greatest of difficulty. Her mother had died of starvation en route and her husband remained behind on duty in Leningrad, never learning that his wife and children survived the war.

It is with the coming of the Germans into Pyatigorsk and the Caucasus, the furthest German penetration into the Soviet Union, that this account begins. She describes the helplessness of the civilian population, ordered by the Soviet authorities to evacuate before the German arrival and yet having no transport or means to do so. Also, a new situation had presented itself and the question facing Elena Skrjabina was how to survive with her two children, how to survive in the most literal sense of the word. For the evacuees from Leningrad and other places had been receiving food in special cafeterias. Now these were closed and absolutely no ration cards were issued. The local population, although suffering greatly, still often had their own gardens or stored food. The new arrivals, however, had nothing.

Elena Skrjabina describes the human side of many of the Germans she met. Yet she also notes some of the dark side of the German occupation and her family's constant fear that the Nazis might discover that her niece's father, her sister-in-law's deceased husband, was Jewish.

As the tide of war turned against the Germans and the Soviets approached Pyatigorsk toward the beginning of 1943, there were new and major worries: the likelihood that her elder son Dima would be shot on sight by the oncoming Reds. The latter had orders to shoot on sight all men between the ages of sixteen and fifty-five, and under the circumstances they most likely would not have bothered to check birth certificates to verify the ages. Indeed what the West often fails to realize is that many ordinary Soviet citizens, in no way Nazi sympathizers or Fascists, fled with the enemy to escape the returning Reds. This is an event almost unprecedented in human history. Millions of people evacuated and retreated with the national and hereditary enemy before the liberation by their own people. There was no other European nation where large numbers of persons willingly left for Germany to avoid their own liberation forces. This is all the more remarkable when it is remembered that there was probably no other nation where the Nazis were as harsh and cruel as they were in Russia.

This is an eyewitness account of the German winter retreat of 1943, of the thousands upon thousands of vehicles jamming the road through the endless, bitterly cold, winter expanse. Again the question was survival. Any false guess, any unwise move, any stay too long in one place or too short in another, could easily have brought starvation. As the present account begins, Elena Skrjabina was living in Pyatigorsk with her two sons, Dima aged fifteen, and Yuri aged five. Arriving there after the perilous and arduous evacuation from Leningrad, she had gone to the apartment of Lyalya, her husband's sister, hoping to find a place to stay. To her great amazement and extreme joy she found her niece Tanya, who had also survived the Leningrad siege and the evacuation to Pyatigorsk. These events were described in her diary, published under the title *Siege and Survival*. In her last diary entry of her book, that for August 9, 1942, she describes Pyatigorsk as the Germans closed in.

August 9   *I awoke at seven o'clock. A complete silence. It is as though last evening trucks had not been pounding over the pavement, as though alarm signals had not been sounding, as though the heavy Red Army boots had not tramped past our windows. And now it seems like a dream. Our charming little garden with its numerous fruit trees is drowned in the gleam of the sun's rays. There is not one cloud in the sky. I sat down on the front porch and did not want to leave as it was so pleasant on this wonderful August morning. Lyalya came to me. She was not going to work any longer. There was not anyone to sew for now. Her clientele had long since departed. Thanks to this silence and peace, one did not want to think about the war and about the German attack. Lyalya, however, insisted that I go with her to cover the little trench in front of the house with boards. This was something which we had long thought of doing but which we had always put off, not wishing to believe in danger. We went, dragging the old gates over there and covered them with earth.*

    The city was beginning to wake up. The housewives were

dragging themselves to market. A group of neighbors went past us happily announcing that railroad cars loaded with flour were standing at the station.

Tanya, Yurochka, and I went toward the market deciding to spend our remaining money to buy some type, any type, of food. There was great animation at the market. Many people had gathered, selling, exchanging. We had just started to purchase our food when a deafening salvo resounded and the entire crowd scattered. We too ran from the marketplace to the city center. After this first salvo nothing followed. The population quickly calmed down, the supposition being expressed that it was possibly the explosion of the power plant which no one was guarding any longer. At this moment another, an extremely loud, artillery shot was heard, then another, a third, a whole cannonade. People began to shout from all sides, "An assault!"

Not knowing what to think, we rushed home. The firing did not cease. Near the house we saw Grandmother and Vera heading toward the trench. This trench seemed like such a fantastically ridiculous cover against such a shelling, a shelling which was shaking the very air, that I shouted to them to run back home. With the entire family and the neighbors, we rushed toward a little wing of the house in the middle of the garden. We closed the windows and doors and set up a genuine barricade of pillows, blankets, and everything we could lay our hands upon. We ourselves lay on the floor. The shelling grew more and more intense. It seemed that it was getting closer and closer. We had the impression that the battle was taking place on our very street. Old Grandmother kept crossing herself, thanking me for having taken her from the street. The noise reached such an intensity that it was difficult to know what was going on. Everything merged into one continuous roar.

Suddenly, everything grew hushed. This silence seemed especially weird, unearthly. Waiting a little while we opened the

*doors and then went out into the garden. It was quiet. The sun
was already setting. The sky was the same clear, blue sky as in the
morning. Only the air was smoky. It was so quiet that even the
leaves on the trees were not rustling. Neither birds nor insects
could be heard. Neither were people to be seen. It seemed as
though a storm had struck and finished everything. We gathered
courage and looked out on the street. At this second we heard the
roar of an approaching tank. It was moving along our fence. On
it were soldiers, in the open, weapons ready. Behind us, a
fifteen-year-old girl, our neighbor's daughter, Milochka, burst
out loudly and joyfully "Ours, ours returned, you see, they are
coming back, they drove back the Germans." Behind the first
tank came another, and another, a whole row. The setting sun
illuminated the black sign of the iron cross. There could no
longer be any doubt. The city had been occupied by the Germans.*

The second volume of Elena Skrjabina's diary begins at this
point, on the evening of the day of the German invasion.

NAMES OF PEOPLE APPEARING IN DIARY

Alexandra   Seamstress in the labor camp near Bendorf. Her fate after the liberation is unknown.

Anna Ivanovna   Neighbor in the refugee camp. She sat with Yuri and told him stories when he was sick.

Bennig   Dima's boss at Krivoi Rog who ordered him a bicycle.

Bolkhovskoi   Actor from the Radlovsky Theater.

Braunstein sisters   Jewish students who hid for a time after the German invasion of Pyatigorsk in the Skrjabin house.

Bruchmann   Plump, friendly German cook. Thanks to his help, Elena Skrjabina was able to save some twenty French prisoners hidden in a cellar at Bendorf. Herr Bruchmann died a few years ago.

Diegel   An officer of Baltic German origin, he pointedly asked about the purchase of horses, thus giving the first hint that the German retreat from Pyatigorsk may be close.

Dima   Elena Skrjabina's eldest son. He completed medical school in Mainz, Germany, and now works in Philadelphia.

Ferger   Paymaster at WIKADO.

Fobke   Commander of the propaganda unit for which Varya Tumanova worked.

Galya   House maid at Krivoi Rog.

Gisela   Neighbor of Elena Skrjabina's friend, Marina. Ran a store in Dresden.

Kommandant Graf   Head of German administration in Brailov.

Grewer   German translator at Bendorf camp. No further news of him.

Gueltz   Replaced Reinhardt as kommandant of the camp at Bendorf.

Josef   German soldier, subordinate of Sulzbach. No further news of him.

Ilya Aranovich   Lyalya's late husband, killed when he was thrown from a train.

Ivan   Lyalya's third husband. Died during World War II.

Ivan Stepanovich   Police chief at Pyatigorsk. Later arrested.

Katya   Young girl who got TB at Bendorf camp.

Colonel Keserling   For a while the commander of WIKADO, the supply section for the German Army.

Keirat   A soldier who transformed their train car into something livable for the journey from Brailov to Krivoi Rog.

Frau Kickel   Manager of the economic administration, food and supply administration in Bendorf. She was continually helping the "Ostarbeiter" (Eastern workers) with coupons for food and clothing. She especially helped the mothers in the camp.

Klava   A camp beauty, competent and witty, sought by the young men of all nationalities at Bendorf.

Klein   Another of the camp kommandants at Bendorf after Reinhardt's departure. He died after the war.

Kleinknecht   Commander of the unit where Nina Pospelova worked as translator at the supply unit in Pyatigorsk.

Mrs. Kolantyrskaya   Communist party official in Leningrad who had kept Elena Skrjabina from having to leave her family and go to school in Siberia.

Kolya   Lyalya's son, killed by a burst of German fire upon the taking of Pyatigorsk.

Kostya   Agreed to go from Bendorf to another camp in exchange for Mariusa's father, thus making possible the reunion between father and daughter.

Dr. Laks   Dr. Laks was commander of the supply unit (WIKADO). He is thought to be still living in Germany.

Levitskys   Celebrated the New Year in 1941 with them. A happy time before the war.

Little Peter   One of the guards at Bendorf.

Luxemburgers (Ketters)   Very fine people with whom Elena Skrjabina became acquainted in Bendorf. The family of Dr. Ketter had been exiled to Germany till the end of the war. Elena Skrjabina met them on a number of occasions after the war. The father, the doctor, died shortly after the end of the hostilities; the eldest daughter died in 1964, the mother a few years later. From this entire charming family there now remain only two children, Paul, Dima's friend, and Jeanne—now married and living in Luxemburg.

Lyalya   Sister of Elena Skrjabina's husband, Sergei, with whom the Skrjabins lived in Pyatigorsk. She returned to Pyatigorsk after the war and is still living there.

Mahomet   Prisoner of war of the Germans who fled along with the Skrjabins to avoid falling into the hands of the returning Reds. Fate unknown.

Maria   Bendorf camp cook who gave large portions of food to her favorite guard, Toni, while others went hungry.

Marina   Friend from Leningrad. Now living in New York after many fantastic experiences.

Mariusa   Finally united with her father at the Bendorf camp.

Martini   Personnel director at the Konkordia plant.

Mattaeus   German Wachtmeister who accompanied Elena Skrjabina when she went to seek German permission to open the café at Pyatigorsk.

Mayer, Paul   Saved Skrjabins from probable starvation in Pyatigorsk. From information received from his mother, he disappeared without trace during the war.

Milochka   A neighbor's daughter.

Miltenberg   Wealthy German officer from Thuringia. Was financially ruined when Reds occupied his property. No further news of him.

Miner   Replaced Keserling as WIKADO commander.

Frau Moyre   After Maria had been caught giving too much food to her favorite guard, Frau Moyre replaced her as a camp cook at Bendorf.

Navrotskaya, Olga   Elena Skrjabina's cousin.

Nikolai   Partisan soldier, one of a group on the outskirts of Pyatigorsk.

Nussbruch   German officer and assistant to Dr. Laks at WIKADO. Elena Skrjabina saw him twice later during the war. There has been no news of him since that time.

Olga   Kitchen worker at Bendorf, feared that she would be taken to work in a bordello. Later covered with tar for dating an Italian.

Olga Aleksandrovna   Agreed to take care of the grandmother when the Skrjabin party evacuated Pyatigorsk.

Paula   Seamstress at Bendorf.

Peter   A fat, viscious Bendorf guard who seems to have had an incomprehensible mixture of cruelty and sentimentality.

Petya   Got into trouble at Bendorf for buying bread on the black market from a Frenchman.

Polya   One of the girls from the factory at Bendorf.

Pospelova, Nina   Leningrader working as secretary to German supply unit, translator. Lost track of her after Pyatigorsk.

Radlovs   Actors from the Radlovsky Theater.

Reinhardt   Kommandant in camp at Bendorf. After the war he was arrested and then released after a trial at which Elena Skrjabina was called to testify. Presumed dead.

Dr. Renzel   Camp physician at Bendorf.

Dr. Riess   Appointed director of Konkordia in 1944. Did a lot of favors for the Russian workers there. Is now living in retirement in Munich.

Herr Roeder   Chief of Bendorf criminal police.

Rudrov   Dima's boss for a while at Krivoi Rog.

Samanov, George   Alexandrovich   Leningrad engineer. In Pyatigorsk he translated for Dr. Laks. Later he worked at Konkordia factory as an engineer and now lives in Philadelphia.

Sasha   A young girl at Bendorf who got TB.

Schreiner   WIKADO officer who offered invaluable help to the Skrjabins. When Elena Skrjabina was sick, he brought Yuri to visit her in the hospital.

Schultz   An officer in the WIKADO.

Schwartz   One of many WIKADO commanders. Gave Dima's boss a tongue lashing for shouting at Dima and pulling a pistol on him.

Sergei   Elena Skrjabina's husband in Leningrad. He survived the war only to die shortly thereafter, never having known that his wife and children had also survived.

Sergei   The husband of one of Elena Skrjabina's cousins. He disappeared after the war.

Shura   Nurse at Bendorf camp who took poison because her boy friend was in love with Klava.

Stahl   With Werner, this German officer found quarters for the Skrjabins at Krivoi Rog.

Sulzbach   German air force officer who helped the Skrjabins evacuate Pyatigorsk. When the German edition of Professor Skrjabina's diary appeared, he attended the publisher's reception in Frankfurt.

Svetlana   Varya Tumanova's sister. Took care of Varya's daughter when Varya was forced to leave Pyatigorsk.

Tamara   The seventeen-year-old girl friend of Dima at Dubovaya Balka.

Tanya   Elena Skrjabina's niece. Evacuated Leningrad, leaving baby daughter behind. Her daughter had been supposed to come on next transport. After the war she met a French career officer of Russian parentage, married him, and now lives in Paris.

Theby   Cordial secretary of the director of Konkordia. She was an amazingly energetic and intelligent woman who continually helped the Skrjabins during their stay in the camp. She is supposed to be still living in a small Rhine town.

Tolbuzina, Marina   Elena Skrjabina's friend who was living in Dresden.

Toni   Camp guard at Bendorf

Tonya   Girl who had a baby at the Bendorf camp.

Traeger   Air force captain in Sulzbach's unit.

Tumanova, Varya   Worked in the propaganda section at Pyatigorsk and wrote many articles that would have infuriated the Red Army. With the Russian Army approaching, she fled with the Skrjabins and the Germans.

Valya   Student from Kharkov who was an inmate at the Bendorf camp.

Vasya   One of the young men at the Bendorf camp.

Vera   Lyalya's daughter who caused great concern when the Germans took Pyatigorsk because her father had been Jewish.

Victor   One of the young men at the factory at Bendorf.

Vladimir   At the time of the opening of the café at Pyatigorsk, Elena Skrjabina speaks of him as "our companion" who speaks no German.

Vanya   Camp inmate, worker, excellent accordian player.

Vanya   Another camp worker, hanged for stealing a pair of shoes during a bombing raid at Bendorf.

Werner   German soldier who found living quarters for Elena Skrjabina at Krivoi Rog.

Wolf   German officer on the WIKADO staff.

Wuergers, Anna   A German woman who helped the "East Workers" and who was very friendly to the Skrjabins at Bendorf. She died a few years ago.

Dr. Wefelsheid   Permanent director of Konkordia who hired the Skrjabins. Elderly, quiet, reserved, Dr. Wefelsheid was very helpful to the Skrjabins and they have the fondest memories of him.

Consul Walter   German consul in Paris whom Miltenberg mistakenly took for von Walther who had been secretary of the German embassy in Moscow and was a very good friend of Elena Skrjabina's cousin, Olga. Consul Walter wrote to Elena Skrjabina once after the war, but then contact was lost.

Dr. von Walther   Had been first secretary of the German embassy in Moscow before the war. After the war he was appointed German ambassador to Moscow. At the present time he is working in Bonn in the department of foreign affairs.

Yuri   The younger of Elena Skrjabina's two sons. Survived the war and immigrated to the United States at age thirteen. Here he completed his higher education. En route from France, where he had attended a conference, to Greece, he was killed in an earthquake in Yugoslavia.

Zina   Kolya's widow, Lyalya's daughter-in-law.

Zubov   Friend of the Skrjabins from Belgium.

NAMES OF PLACES APPEARING IN DIARY

Armavir Soviet city in Caucasus. The population in 1939 was 84,000. The present population is 155,000.

Aschaffenburg Because of an air attack on Frankfurt, the Skrjabins' train had to be rerouted to this German city as they were on their way to Bendorf.

Azov, Sea of Shallow sea connected by narrow straits to Black Sea. The Don flows into this sea, which is located to the east of the Crimea.

Bad Ems A beautiful city on the Rhine that the Skrjabins visited from Bendorf.

Baku Large Soviet city on the Caspian Sea in the oil region. The population in 1939 was 773,000. In 1974 it was 1.4 million.

Bendorf Small German city of about 12,000 on the Rhine near Koblenz. It was the site of the Konkordia factory and the camp where the Skrjabins worked and lived.

Brailov Small city about 30 miles from Vinnitsa. This was in an area that had a large Jewish population. It suffered extremely during Nazi occupation.

Breslau Polish city where Elena Skrjabina had to change trains when she went to Bendorf.

Chaltyr Village Small village where the Skrjabins spent the night and most of the day on the evacuation from Pyatigorsk.

Cherepovets City along the rail evacuation line from Leningrad. Here Elena Skrjabina's mother died during the evacuation, as did thousands of other weakened Leningraders. In 1939 the population was 32,000.

Crimea Famous peninsula in the Black Sea. Since the south side of the mountains is shielded from the north winds, parts of the Crimea were regarded as something of a Russian Riviera.

Dneprodzerzhinsk   Until 1936 this city was named Kamenskoye and had about 148,000 inhabitants prior to the war. It is an industrial center on the lower Dniepr.

Dneproges   Short for Dniepr hydroelectric station built between 1927–1933.

Dnepropetrovsk   Site of famous dam built by Soviets during the first five-year plan. Blown up to prevent it from falling into hands of advancing Germans, it was subsequently rebuilt. The city had a population of 528,000 in 1939 and by 1974 had over 900,000.

Dresden   Large city in Saxony in present-day East Germany (DDR). This city suffered what some believe to be the highest death toll from a bombing raid in history, higher even than that of Hiroshima and Nagasaki.

Dubovaya Balka   Worker suburb of Krivoi Rog.

Essentuki   The city where the Braunstein sisters, Jewish students hiding with the Skrjabins, had friends who would take them in after the German invasion of Pyatigorsk.

Goryachevodsk   Literally "Hot Waters," a Caucasian spa near Pyatigorsk.

Karer   A small railroad village on the evacuation route from Pyatigorsk.

Karlsruhe   Germany city of about a quarter of a million inhabitants between Frankfurt and Switzerland.

Kavkazkaya   Cossack settlement or stanitsa located on the right bank of the Kuban River on the rail line from Krasnodar to Stavropol. In the 1920s this city had a population of about 10,000.

Kharkov   Second most populous city of the Ukraine. Captured by Germans in 1941, lost by them, then recaptured in early 1943 before it was again taken by the Reds. Population in 1939 was 840,000, presently 1.3 million.

Kiev   Capital of the Ukraine, sometimes called the "mother of Russian cities." Center of old Russian culture. Population in 1939 was 851,000. By 1974 it had more than doubled.

Kirovograd   Until 1934 it was Elizavetograd. It was renamed in honor
of the murdered Kirov. It is an important commerce center in
the Ukraine; the population in 1939 was 103,000, presently over
200,000.

Kislovodsk   Where the Jewish students, the Braunstein sisters, were
working as translators for a German unit.

Klievatka   Where Varya Tumanova was invited to manage a casino.

Koblenz   Germany city at the confluence of the Rhine and the
Moselle, less than seven miles from Bendorf.

Kovel   City in the Ukrainian section of the USSR in Volhynia. Prior
to World War II the population was largely Jewish. Between
1920–1939 it was under Poland but was annexed by the Soviet
Union as a result of the Hitler-Stalin pact.

Krasnodar   Formerly Ekaterinodar (Katherine's gift), this is a large
city in the Caucasus. The population in 1939 was 193,000.

Kremenczuk   Ukrainian industrial city near Poltava. Population in
1939 was 90,000.

Krivoi Rog   Important metallurgical center in the Ukraine. In 1939
the population was 192,000. By 1974 it had risen to over 600,000.

Ladozhskaya   A cossack stanitsa on the evacuation route from
Pyatigorsk.

Lavra   Famous Kievan cave monastery, the oldest in Russia.

Lodz   Large and important Polish manufacturing and industrial center, which the Germans renamed Litzmannstadt.

Lublin   Polish city about 105 miles southeast of Warsaw. Site of
infamous Nazi concentration camp at Maidanek. It was in this
city that the Soviets set up a Polish government during World
War II.

Mariupol   Renamed Zhdanov in 1948. Important port on the Sea of
Azov, which in 1939 had a population of 222,000

Melitopol   The propaganda unit offered to take the Skrjabins to this
city from Mariupol, but they decided not to go.

Mineralnyie Vody   Literally "Mineral Waters," this is a famous

Caucasian spa near Pyatigorsk. In 1939 it had a population of 31,000.

Nal'chik   Capital of Kabardian USSR in Central Caucasus. Located in the Terek River basin, it had a population of 48,000 in 1939.

Neuwied   A city only nine kilometers from Bendorf. Its bombing caused the Skrjabins great uneasiness.

Nikolaevka   A village fifteen kilometers from Pyatigorsk.

Nova-Ukrainka   Where the friendly and helpful German officer, Schreiner, was sent from Krivoi Rog.

Odessa   Largest Russian port on the Black Sea. Occupied by the Rumanians during World War II.

Orekhov   The first stop when the Skrjabins evacuated Mariupol with the WIKADO.

Poltava   Famous Ukrainian city, the site of an extremely important battle in 1709 when Peter the Great defeated the Swedes. Regional capital on a Dniepr tributary.

Protchnookopskaya   Cossack village.

Pyatigorsk   The Russian spa in the Caucasus where the Skrjabins hoped to sit out the war. It was taken by the Germans August 9, 1942. It was from this city that the Skrjabins evacuated with the Germans at the approach of the Red Army.

Radom   Polish city, one of the stations along the way to Germany.

Rostov   Important Russian industrial city on the Don River by the Sea of Azov. Changed hands four times during World War II. The population in 1939 was 510,000.

Saksagan   A large village on the evacuation route from Pyatigorsk.

Sayn   Many people evacuated to this Rhineland city after the bombing of Bendorf.

Shepetovka   A large settlement on the border between Russia and Poland.

Skarzysko Kamienna   Polish city some twenty miles north by northeast of Kielce. It has a population of approximately 15,000.

Thuringia   Kommandant Klein at Bendorf announced to the inmates of the camp that if the Anglo-Americans approached too closely, they would have to go on foot to Thuringia, a central German province.

Tuszyn   Small flour mill town near Lodz, Poland, with a population of 4,000.

Uman   Russian city, 53,000 in 1962.

Vinnitsa   District capital in the USSR on the Volhynia plateau near Rumania.

Zaporozhye   Historically famous as a Cossack stronghold on the Dniepr River south of Kiev. An important industrial center with a population of 289,000 in 1939, it had a population of over 700,000 in 1974.

Zhmerinka   Ukranian town under Rumanian administration. Elena Skrjabina was in the hospital there while the family was staying in Brailov.

After

Leningrad

The Germans in the Caucasus

Ten O'clock in the Evening, August 9, 1942   We* returned to our apartment. There we found two girls, students from my institute who twice had tried to get away, but hadn't succeeded. You can't get far on foot with a knapsack on your back. Nonetheless, the teacher who was with them had managed to get a ride on a wagon, but the people on the wagon would not take three. The girls were very alarmed. Rumors about Nazi measures against the Jews were very persistent. They had come to us since they were afraid to remain in Goryachevodsk, where they had lived and where everybody knew them. They felt it was less dangerous at our place. Lyalya was very uneasy. To refuse under such circumstances was impossible, but to give shelter was dangerous. Now she was especially afraid for her own daughter, Vera, as the presence of these girls might bring

---

*At this time Elena Skrjabina had evacuated besieged and starving Leningrad and was living in Pyatigorsk with her two sons, Yuri, five, and Dima, fourteen. In Pyatigorsk she was staying with her husband's sister, Lyalya, and the latter's husband, Ivan, son Kolya, and Kolya's wife, Zina. Tanya, Elena Skrjabina's niece from Leningrad, had managed to leave the starving city and was also living with them. Just before the war interfered, Elena Skrjabina had resumed her studies and was working toward an advanced degree in French at the Leningrad Institute of Foreign Languages.—Ed.

suspicion onto her house. For the time being we placed them in the little pantry, where a few days ago, alarmed by Soviet propaganda, we had raised the floor boards and hidden our few edible supplies. The door to the pantry is right next to the front entrance and would scarcely be noticed, since there are all types of things piled up around it. Although we had convinced ourselves of this, nonetheless it seemed, as it always does when you want to hide something especially well, that the selected place was not at all reliable. We couldn't think of any other place, since the entire apartment was open and resembled a passageway.

We began to look out the windows to see what was happening in the city.

After just a few hours Pyatigorsk had already completely changed. On every corner signs and pointers had sprung up. Cars and motorcycles were flashing by. From everywhere could be heard loud talking, not at all resembling the songlike South-Russian speech. Now and then there was firing and a shell would whistle past. The civilian population was forbidden to go out on the streets.

August 10, 1942   Early in the morning we were awakened by loud voices under our windows. It seemed that the Germans were very dissatisfied with something and therefore were shouting. No matter how we tried, we could pick up only an occasional word. Traffic was getting heavier with each passing hour. New units were arriving constantly. Several trucks entered our small orchard and broke our wonderful fruit trees whose very special fruit, plums, had just ripened. A young German, apparently a supply sergeant, entered our apartment and announced to us that they were occupying the large room which had served us both as a living room and a dining room and in which the boys and I slept. They allowed us to spend nights in it as before, since the office would be closed at five o'clock. There could be no thought of objections. The Germans immediately began getting themselves set up, and in a very little while the room was transformed into a real office. In order not to be seen, we sat down in the two little rooms along the corridor. The question of the two students, the Braunstein sisters, was becoming more and more complicated. From seven till five they were cut off from the whole world and we could not bring them food. Shooting was still going on. From the conversations of the Germans we understood that Red Army men had taken up positions in Goryachevodsk and from there they were shelling the city. The first day of the German occupation was nearing its end.

August 11, 1942   We weren't able to fall asleep easily last night. An explosion of unusual force shook our house; right after it came a second and a third. We all threw ourselves on the floor in order to avoid the windows, the glass of which shuddered and threatened to come flying out at any moment. All of us crawled into the small vestibule and waited there for whatever would come. From the street we heard shouts and an uninterrupted rumble of explosions. The Germans, who had set themselves up in our orchard, were also crouching down and crawling about; there was a constant uneasy muttering among them. The impression that the bombardment was again beginning did not leave us. The students also came out of their hiding place and took their places in the dark entryway. At that time, when, as a result of the unbearable noise of the explosions, it seemed that the entire world was coming to an end, they had no time to worry about their Jewish origin. In two hours everything grew silent, but there could no longer be any thought about sleep. For some reason we were all expecting something to happen. Only toward morning, when the young people were again sleeping soundly, my sister-in-law and I went walking around like ghosts, listening to everything that was taking place on the streets.

August 12, 1942   The reason for last night's shelling, which had panicked us, has been cleared up. Red soldiers in Goryachevodsk were firing the famous Katusha rockets.* They were soon driven from their ambush by German units. Today, for the first time, we decided to go out on the streets. Everywhere there was evidence of the fighting. On the corner of Kochura Street the body of a dead young Russian soldier was lying near a blown-up car. Nobody had buried him. Obviously the Russians were afraid and the Germans were occupied with their own affairs. A professor whom we had known from Leningrad approached us along with several of his students. A young German ordered them to bury the dead one. The Russians, together with the Germans, dug a grave right there on the corner and placed the corpse into it. The further we went, the more dead we came across. Apparently the fighting had been taking place on the streets at the very time that we were sitting barricaded in the apartment wing.

We returned home, where sorrowful news was awaiting us. Ivan, Lyalya's husband, had arrived from the hospital, frightened to death. Stammering and shaking all over, he told us that Lyalya's son, Kolya, had died. When the attack had begun and the first Germans had reached the hospital fence, many of the hospital patients, seeking safety, had thrown themselves into the newly dug trenches in the garden. Ivan had remained in the hospital corridor, and had dropped to the floor under the windows. Kolya did not follow his example and had hidden with the others in the trench. A Red Army man had jumped in there

*Soviet antitank rockets.—Ed.

with the patients and continued to fire his rifle at the approaching Germans. A German fired a burst from his machine gun, killing Kolya and a young actor from the Leningrad Radlovsky theater who had been praying for the arrival of the Germans so that he could go to the Ukraine, to which his wife and child had been evacuated earlier. Two nurses who were some distance from the trench survived, and they had given the details of this tragic event.

At home the mood is extremely depressing. Kolya's mother and wife are especially grieving. All of us are sorry about Kolya, an extremely nice boy whom everyone loved. Although we tried very carefully to hide this, somehow the Germans found out what had occurred. They expressed their sympathy to his mother and wife. There was no noticeable animosity.

August 13, 1942   Today our neighbors told how the Germans had opened the prisons. However, all the inmates had been killed before the entry of the Germans and the bodies had been doused with lime. In the prison office were found the papers of the prisoners and some of their possessions. Now the relatives are being informed. As soon as the martial law is lifted, the corpses are to be identified and buried. How fortunate it was that none of us was in jail!

August 15, 1942   Since the shelling still continued and since the city had been placed under martial law, we could not get to the hospital where Kolya was lying. Lyalya wanted to find his body in order to bury it in the cemetery. Today finally the Germans gave us permission to go there. It was quiet in the city. Who was going to go? Neither his mother nor his wife was in any shape to go. Ivan was scared to death to stick his nose out in the street. Tanya and I decided to go. We were able to find a fellow who undertook to dig up the whole trench and find Kolya among the dead. The search took two hours. Far more persons had perished than we had understood from the words of the nurses. It was difficult for us to recognize Kolya, since the body had begun to decompose during the week, largely because of the terrible heat. We were able to recognize him because of several marks. His remains were placed into a coffin and the coffin put in the hospital mortuary. Tomorrow will be the burial.

August 16, 1942   Today our Kolya was buried. With the help of an officer from that unit at our place, we had easily obtained permission to bury him in the family crypt. Lyalya's deceased husband, Ilya Aranovich, who had been thrown from a train three years ago, and Kolya's and Zina's little daughter, who had died last winter, were also in that vault. We were all so sorry for Kolya. He had been so sure that the Germans would not reach the Caucasus and had not wanted to evacuate into the unknown. And now he himself was the first victim. I am ashamed to admit it, but I kept thinking, "Why Kolya and not Ivan?" And I think I was not the only one with that thought.

August 17, 1942   Our greatest worry was the students living in our pantry. They could not stay there forever. Yesterday evening when the office was closed they came to us and told us that they had decided to leave. They knew someone in Essentuki whom they could count on. It's difficult to give advice under such circumstances. When it had become completely dark, they left their refuge. I hope that everything comes out all right. It does not appear that the German units which we saw are very interested in the Jewish question. The 777 Column which has set itself up in our orchard and in the basement is for the most part favorably disposed toward us. The soldiers begin washing in the early morning. This is an endless procedure and takes place in the yard by the well pump. After that they have breakfast in the garden. Watching them through the window we are amazed at the abundance of food and by the prevailing cleanliness and order. Immediately after breakfast everybody sets off to work. This one repairs cars; that one washes them; another one is busy with moving supplies, and yet another is busy with various reports and calculations. The nicest of them all, Paul, is the director of the unit's supplies. He is tall, blond and blue-eyed, always cheerful and well-inclined toward everyone. It's surprising that he wasn't taken into the SS; indeed, that's the physical type they select, so we're told.

August 18, 1942   Today there was an incident with this Paul. He asked me for the keys to the pantry. Although the girls are no longer there, my heart was pounding from fear that he had somehow found out about our buried treasures and that now would come the reckoning for our crimes. I gave him the keys and told Lyalya about what had happened. We sat and waited. Soon he gave me back the keys, not saying a word. I ran to the pantry and stopped. There were heaps of foods on the tables and on the shelves. Nonetheless, I was still doubtful of our good fortune. I asked Paul whether they were requisitioning our pantry. He replied that he had noticed that we were hungry and that he had brought all those provisions for us.*

August 19, 1942   On the way to the market to buy vegetables and cabbage, both of which are available for very high prices, I saw a scene which moved me very much. Two troikas which were standing in front of the church all decked out in ribbons had just started up. A young couple was sitting in the first troika.

---

*Elena Skrjabina and her relatives had virtually exhausted the little supply of food they had stored and might have starved had this soldier, Paul Mayer, not realized their predicament and saved them.—Ed.

Living in Leningrad in 1939 Elena Skrjabina, then thirty-three, seemed safe from the war because Russia and Germany had just astonished the world by signing a nonagression pact.

The Germans had opened the churches almost immediately after taking the city. There were several other curious spectators standing with me near the church gates, obviously just as enthused about the unaccustomed spectacle as I was, "They are finally marrying again like Christians and not like dogs," was one commentary, and other remarks sounded very similar.

August 20, 1942   Gradually we are getting used to the new conditions of life. A Leningrader, an engineer by profession, suggested to us that we open a café jointly. This idea appealed to us all.*

---

*The Germans did not issue ration cards when they entered the city. The local populace, many of whom had their own gardens or minor supplies of food, were

August 22, 1942   To open a café you need the permission of the German command and the Russian administration. I asked the German Wachtmeister Matthaeus to accompany me when I went to the Russian authorities. There were so many different marks and insignias on his sleeve that our people, who are still in awe of the Germans and are not familiar with the foreign military ranks, could easily take him for a high and important officer. Matthaeus came with me quite readily, and thus I received permission right on the spot.

It was difficult, however, to get a place for the café. The one we had wanted had already been claimed by the Field Gendarmerie. It seems likely that we can get a former perfume shop in our neighborhood. This store does not quite meet our requirements. There are shop tables and counters with glass doors. Behind the shop is a room and a kitchen. The various odors which are present in the rooms are very unpleasant. Everything smells of perfume, eau de cologne, and soap. For other purposes this might be very good. However, what would happen if all our cakes and pastries were to take on the aroma of "Red Moscow" (a famous perfume)?

August 28, 1942   This morning our Column 777 was surprised by the order to move on. Everything seemed empty in the house and garden. It's too bad. We had become used to them, and they didn't bother us. On the contrary, we felt secure under their protection, and we had counted on their assistance in opening the café. It is not at all certain who will replace them. It is said that the advance combat units are the best.

---

not immediately as severely affected by the food shortage as the evacuees. The new arrivals, who had been receiving food at specially established eating halls and from special cards, were in a very precarious situation. If they did not find some way of earning enough to get food on the free market, they would simply have starved.

At the front the Germans were continuing their advance into the Caucasus, reaching Mt. Elbrus, Europe's highest peak, the next day.—Ed.

Zina is crying. Blue-eyed Paul had done her good and she seems thereby to have pretty much forgotten Kolya.

September 1, 1942   The café is open. No one had the faintest idea how to run such a business. There was still no stove in the kitchen, so we baked at home in the evening. In the morning we carried our entire production to the café. The city administration had given us twenty chairs and four small tables. We placed flowers on the tables, and since the sign we had ordered was not ready yet, we painted on a sheet of paper in both Russian and German, "Café Open." We hung this on the door and began to wait. Time passed. No one came. Almost simultaneously we all had the same idea: "What if nobody would come?" At that very moment we noticed a group of German officers coming from the other side of the street. Everybody became confused; the girls hid in the back rooms, imploring Dima to serve the customers. The first confusion passed quickly. A constant stream of customers came, and by twelve o'clock we had sold out our entire supply. This success encouraged us greatly.

September 4, 1942   Now all our interests are centered in the café. Lyalya, Dima, and I spend the entire day there. The girls work in shifts. Ivan runs to the markets and in the evening checks the accounts. This is his favorite occupation. He gets on all our nerves. He doesn't trust anyone and is certain that we are all mistaken in our figures. He has such a strange appearance that we can't let him serve the customers.* As soon as he returns from the market, we think up some other task for him to do so as to get him out of the café. Yesterday a colonel, pointing to Ivan, asked me, "Is that your cook?" I nodded yes.

*Ivan was small, not at all good looking, but above all, he always looked so frightened and pitiful that he was not a good advertisement for any business.—Ed.

September 7, 1942   The repair is finally finished. In the kitchen a fine new stove has been set up. We have hired a pastry baker. All the shelves are filled with pies and baked goods of the most varied types, showing the culinary art of our chef. However, the clientele is so large that we could double or even triple our production. There are great difficulties with the purchase of the necessary products. Dima and Ivan are already at the market at six o'clock in the morning. If they arrive later it's already too late to get anything. We have to get permission from the German quartermaster command to go for provisions to Nal'chik, where the supply is greater. Pyatigorsk is overcrowded both with military units and evacuees. Here there are many fine buildings, formerly sanatoria, where various military units are quartered. Restaurants, cafés and stores are being opened. Life is bubbling.

Many Russians, especially evacuees from Leningrad, are visiting our café. All of these people, who were starving during the time of the blockade, have not seen such pastries for a long time, and are enjoying at our place all these masterpieces of our baker. He was, by the way, famous even in prerevolutionary Pyatigorsk, when the "cream" of Petersburg and Moscow society would come here.

September 9, 1942   Today I went to WIKADO* This was the German supply section. We had had a family meeting at which I had been chosen to go since neither Lyalya nor our companion, Vladimir, knew a word of German. En route I was recalling all the tricks to which I had resorted with my German teacher when, out of patriotic reasons, I had not wanted at the time of the First World War to learn German. How useful a good knowledge of German would be now!

*Wirtschafts Komando, a command, an economic unit, essentially a supply unit, but it also had to do with allocations for civilians in occupied areas.—Ed.

By the office there were already many people waiting. They were all owners of small enterprises which had arisen since the German entry. All of them were extremely agitated and didn't dare enter this holy "temple." Since I did not wish to get infected by their mood, I suggested to them that I go in first. Everybody agreed immediately; I entered, and was pleasantly impressed by what I saw. To the right of me a young man, apparently a Russian translator, got up and walked toward me, asking me for what purpose I was there. Further back in the room, at a desk, was sitting the extremely young unit commander, that very dreaded Doctor Laks, before whom all the merchants of Pyatigorsk trembled. I didn't see anything to be dreaded in him, and, not availing myself of the interpreter, went directly to Dr. Laks. He, first explaining the situation, told me that I could return in several days and receive permission for the trip. I invited them both to come visit our café and returned home delighted with the success of my mission.

September 12, 1942　　I am so busy with the café that I don't have time for anything personal. I don't even get a chance to write the daily events in my diary. Every day new people come to our café, and we often meet old friends whom we have not seen for a long time. The clients are attracted to our café by the fine delicacies, the pretty waitresses, and the easy, relaxed atmosphere. I am always especially happy when our Leningraders come. The Radlovs, Bolkhovskoi and other actors of the Radlovsky Theater are frequent guests. With them we can speak about the old days. Everything that had been happening before the war seemed to us now so bright and happy, and all of these memories are bound up with our beloved city. The Neva,* the palaces, the white nights—where is there anything like it? Al-

---

*The Neva is for Russia what the Thames is for Britain or the Seine for France; it is the river on which Leningrad is located.—Ed.

though things are going very well at the present in Pyatigorsk, we all long to be back there.

Our pastry baker has a helper now; she makes the Caucasian specialties which are so popular. In the back room Lyalya receives the most important personalities of the entire city, as she puts it: the police chief and the chairman of the City Council (*Gorsoviet*). She doesn't like it when I sit down with my Leningraders and don't translate for her with influential Germans. For her, of course, Leningraders are nothing special. Tanya and I are thinking about the possibility of finding ourselves an apartment; then it would be much easier for us to invite whomever we want, and not receive them in the café.

September 13, 1942   Except for the apartment, we have resumed a more or less normal life. To live behind a screen in the dining room since work began in the café is almost unthinkable, and Yuri and I have moved into a wing with the neighbors. There also it is not calm. There are five of us in two rooms, and there is no place to put our things. They are strewn everywhere. Sometimes passing units requisition one of the rooms for the night for officers. Then it is very crowded. We are looking very hard for an apartment.

September 25, 1942   We finally moved to a real apartment which had belonged to Communists who fled Pyatigorsk and had been requisitioned by the city administration. The chief of police, a very suspicious type, by the way, helped us get the apartment. Everywhere it is the same. Everything is possible if you know the right people. Dima, Yurochka, and Tanya came. The latter has decided to live with us. Lyalya is extremely dissatisfied with this, but, of course, she doesn't want to force Tanya to remain. Since we don't have to prepare meals at home, we don't especially miss not having a kitchen in the apartment. In one of the two rooms there is a stove on which it is possible to cook; however, since the room is large we screened it off and set up a corner for Dima, and the other part serves as dining room and living room. The three of us, Yuri, Tanya, and I, are in the second room, also of good size. It is very difficult to imagine a better situation.

September 28, 1942   Today our peaceful and happy mood was suddenly destroyed by an extremely unpleasant event. About three o'clock in the afternoon, just when business in the café was at its peak, Soviet airplanes attacked. There was no warning whatsoever. A deafening explosion resounded. There was a shower of breaking glass, and everybody threw himself onto the floor. The whistle of the hurtling bombs, the roar of the explosions and the resulting destruction, the shouts for help from the street, all merged into one uninterrupted howl. It continued not very long at all; however, at the time it seemed an eternity. When everything had grown quiet, our café presented a very sad spectacle. Everything down to the last window had been blown out. Even the sign which we had just received a few days ago and which we had admired was dangling pitifully on one hook. Only two letters remained intact. Since all the windows were broken, we had to send all our guests away. Only toward evening had we finished with the cleaning up and boarded up the windows.

One cannot forget that the war is far from being over. Obviously, military activity is very close. The Germans obviously don't like to talk about that. But this raid, without any sort of resistance on their part, seems extremely suspicious. Most likely Red units are firmly established in the mountains.

September 29, 1942   Yesterday evening we went through the city to look over the damage. The bombs had, for the most part, hit the center of town. There had been numerous pedestrians on the boulevard, and many of them had been killed or wounded. Some houses had been completely destroyed; others were severely damaged; the window panes in the entire area had been broken. Further out there was no damage. Fortunately our apartment did not suffer at all. Till yesterday one or two Soviet planes would occasionally approach the outskirts of the city and hurriedly fly away after hastily dropping their bombs. Till now we had always considered our own air force insignificant, and the German defense as far superior. Now, however, our faith in the security of Pyatigorsk has been shaken.

October 1, 1942   All the café repair work has now been finished. When one is able to pay with food there is no delay either with workers or with materials. Money is simply paper which has lost all its value. The doors are again open and the café is overflowing. We have become acquainted with a new officer named Sulzbach. He is the commander of the air defense forces. They are stationed some fifteen kilometers from Pyatigorsk in the village of Nikolaevka. He assures us that there is nothing to be uneasy about, and that Soviet planes will no longer get through to the city. Involuntarily I am reminded of similar assurances of Soviet propaganda in Leningrad. Having been deceived then, I am very skeptical now. However, I don't let on that I have any doubts about the organizational ability and military might of the Germans.

October 3, 1942   I received from WIKADO and Dr. Laks permission to go for flour and can leave tomorrow in a German car. Sulzbach dropped by again and invited us to a party in his unit. Since I refused because of lack of time, he promised to come for Tanya, for whom this was a great pleasure. This officer is very nice and always happy. When he's around we forget that the war is not far away and who knows what further dangers might threaten us.

October 5, 1942   Yesterday I spent the entire day in Nal'chik. The results were excellent. We brought back a few sacks of flour and everything went well. The population there is very calm, and everyone maintains that Soviet forces haven't been in the area for a long time.

Elena Skrjabina often visited this marketplace to procure supplies for the café in Pyatigorsk.

October 6, 1942   The atmosphere around us has been darkened, however, by strange types of rumors circulating in the city about the fate of the Jews. A week ago I had given my jumper to be taken in to a Jewish woman who was a talented seamstress. Today I dropped by for the fitting, as we had arranged. But she appeared not to be at home. Her neighbors informed me with a mysterious look that she had been taken away during the night. Similar stories are to be heard about one of the German language teachers of our Leningrad Pedagogical Institute. We are informed only from rumors and know nothing definite. However, the Soviet radio broadcasts about German measures against the Jews come to mind.

A few hours after I had heard all of this, I was walking down the street and a few steps from our café, which was across from the German Kommandatura, I noticed an open car and in it our two friends, the Braunstein sisters, who had been hiding in our pantry the first days of the German occupation. It turned out that they were working as translators in a German unit in Kislovodsk. They felt fine and were receiving excellent rations and a salary. I didn't tell them a thing about my doubts. What sense is there in frightening them? There is no way out for them, and perhaps it is safer for them in the very mouth of the lions. Their boldness might save them. Their passports? Indeed, these could have been lost in the very first days of chaos. Let's pray that nobody reports them. People are mean and envious of others' good fortune.

October 10, 1942   All the Jews who registered at the Kommandatura, in accordance with a German edict, have been transported somewhere. Those who did not appear and purposely lost their documents and moved to smaller places where nobody knows them did the right thing. Indeed, the most dangerous persons are those who are trying to ingratiate themselves with the Germans. These, for the most part, are the ones who are occupying responsible positions in the police, in the Kommandatura, and in the city government. Thus, for example, I don't trust the police chief and his crowd one iota. For me he is a provocateur of the purest type. Lyalya is with him often, and I cannot tell her my opinion about this bandit. We are kept informed of events by a Jew who is married to a Russian who often comes to our place. For the time being, he says, there is no danger either to the spouses in a mixed marriage or to the children of such marriages. They are not even being called to register. This is a good sign. Apparently he is right, but perhaps they will not be bothered only for the time being. Who can vouch for anything?

October 13, 1942   Materially we are now living as well as we ever have. True, we work a great deal, but on the other hand the results are visible. We are very satisfied with our apartment. Dima buys books, which interest him more than anything else. He buys them not only for himself but also for Yuri, and our library is growing. Many inhabitants are forced to sell both their furniture and their books in order to survive the difficult times, for the prices for food in the market are still very high, and there is no food in the stores. Yuri spends the days with his new governess, and he, too, is enjoying life. Our young girls flirt with the customers at the café. A young Russian is courting Verochka. When he came the first day and left Vera, who had served him, a tip of twenty marks,* everybody was struck by this unusual sum, but no one knew who or what he was. Now it's turned out that he is the son of emigrants who left Russia in 1918 and he has spent his entire life in Prague. At the outbreak of the war, this young fellow entered the German army and thus came to the Caucasus. He has become a constant visitor. There are also other Russians who come. Usually they serve as special guides, thanks to their knowledge of the Russian language. All of these are persons who left Russia long ago and believe that the Germans will liberate the country from the Communists.

*The mark in 1977 was worth about forty cents.—Ed.

October 14, 1942   It is obvious that there is never complete peace in life. It seems as though everything has been arranged; the family is secure, we've even forgotten about hunger, but nonetheless something keeps weighing on my heart. The war is still raging at full intensity. Leningrad is in the vise. There is, of course, absolutely no news about my husband and friends who remained there. The future is very murky. Apparently the Soviet forces have retreated into the depths of the Caucasus. There are almost no air raids. Artillery fire hasn't been heard for a long time. It is said that the Soviets have dug in in the mountains, from which it will be difficult to dislodge them. It appears as though the war will drag on. Several Leningraders who are working as translators often come and tell me various rumors. At first the Germans were convinced that they would have a triumphal march through the Caucasus and that the war would end with the taking of Baku. Now the picture is changing. And this confidence has been shaken.

October 16, 1942   About two hours ago a strange woman dropped in. She was very elegant and pretty, and introduced herself as a translator for the Kislovodsk kommandant. She ordered some pies for the forthcoming holiday and said that she, too, was one of the evacuees from Leningrad. However, no one among the Leningraders who were in the café at the time knew her. She asked Lyalya to go with her into one of the back rooms so that no one could hear their conversations. It turned out later that she had asked a number of questions about Jews who were living in Pyatigorsk. We all had the impression that she was a spy. I feel that espionage, about which I had laughed when I was in Leningrad at the beginning of the war, is now overtaking even me.

October 18, 1942   To outward appearances, our café seems to be running beautifully, and we are getting wealthier with each day. The reality is quite different. If we don't receive a large loan from the bank we won't even be able to pay our debts. It turns out that we are poor business people. The reasons are easy enough to find. First of all, everyone who is at all sharp is stealing. The cook, his assistant, the dishwasher, all go home in the evening with such packages that it is even painful for us, the owners, to look. Secondly, we are all too generous in treating our clients. With no hesitation at all, the girls pour in genuine coffee for all their admirers instead of the intended substitute (ersatz) coffee. They also try not to write down the pastries that these suitors eat. And since they each have a number of suitors, the losses to us are quite considerable. Lyalya is also constantly and diligently serving the VIPs—without remuneration, of course. I am at fault in connection with the Leningraders. It seems to me that they are far more deserving than the others. Many of them don't have the means with which to pay the fantastic sums which we have to ask for our products. We have to take immediate steps or else the whole thing will go down the drain.

October 24, 1942   A speculator of extremely suspicious appearance appeared today and sold us a few sacks of genuine coffee; he says it's Turkish. Everything is possible. The taste is good, but the price is fantastic. Lyalya maintains that it is impossible to give our guests the coffee which is available on the open market.

October 26, 1942   Today we found out that the Germans arrested the police commander. Apparently he had been left behind here with definite missions. Lyalya is now terrified, since everyone knew about their good relationship. In the course of these last two months his bearded face was a constant accessory in our café. We also received our apartment through his influence. It is better if no one knows about it. Lyalya has many enemies among the population. Everyone tries to gain some benefit from our café. Some offer us their pastry for sale; others want to work for us, and still others only want to eat there. Lyalya is therefore forced to turn many away. This causes irritation, as a rule, and there are even those who don't hesitate to tell her very unpleasant things straight to her face. In these troubled times, such misunderstandings are very unnerving. It is impossible to avoid them. Ivan causes the most worry. He has already begun to try to persuade us to move to another city, under the pretext of hiding Vera. In reality, however, he is deathly afraid of the consequences of his friendship with the police chief, before whom he had kow-towed as much as he could during these two months. In this atmosphere of tension, his forebodings and dire predictions are especially unnerving.

October 28, 1942   Herr Nussbruch, a regular guest of the café and Dr. Laks' deputy in the WIKADO protects our enterprise and understands our difficult position. Recently he recommended that we speak with Dr. Laks about a possible loan and brought the latter with him to the café.

Apparently he had already spoken with him about our situation. At any rate we did not have to speak very long with him. Dr. Laks will help us get a loan for fifty thousand marks which we will have to pay back in the course of this coming year. We happily agreed to this.

November 3, 1942   Again the situation has been improved. The loan saved us. We bought all sorts of foods, enough to last us the winter. Our general mood has also improved. One thing still bothers us, however, and that is the story about the police chief. The jail is located in the yard behind the German Kommandatura, almost right across the street from our café. For reasons completely incomprehensible to us, the arrested Ivan Stepanovich is allowed to come twice a day—under guard, of course—to eat lunch and supper at our place. This is so incomprehensible that I don't even try to understand it. How strange the Germans act at times. Who ever heard of the NKVD* allowing prisoners to eat in a restaurant! And he still acts extremely self-assured, and if at the time of his arrival neither Lyalya nor I is there to have his meal served right away, he expresses his displeasure. The guards who bring him enjoy the same privileges as he does, and apparently are quite satisfied with these excursions to the restaurant. They probably have received special instructions from the kommandant, and we don't dare object, even though such visitations are extremely unpleasant for us.

November 10, 1942   The most disturbing question for all the inhabitants of Pyatigorsk, and us too, is the question about mixed marriages. We finally asked the Germans. They either really don't know or don't wish to say. Even Nussbruch is silent. I'll grant that they really don't know. Indeed, did we simple mortals in the USSR know anything about what preparations were being made "above?"

We are living in complete ignorance of what is happening around us; whether the Germans have gone far into the Caucasus, what is happening on other fronts, on whose side fortune is at the present—all this is shrouded in mystery. We feed on rumors from the girls, from the secretaries, and from Russian visitors to the café who are inclined to speak about such topics. We are in no way able to judge what is true and what is not.

*This is the Soviet equivalent of the Gestapo. The letters stand for People's Commissariat of Internal Affairs, which is a nice euphemism.—Ed.

November 15, 1942   A large part of the population of Pyatigorsk has fully "accepted" the German occupation. The main reason is that the Germans have given wide freedom to individual initiative. Not only are private enterprises flourishing, but even individuals. Some bake *pirozhki** and sell them at the market; others present their wares in restaurants and cafés, while still others work as waitresses and cooks in those very restaurants. Many sell kvass and mineral water in the kiosks. Shoemakers have opened shops. Those who know German work in German offices as translators or messengers and receive food rations, in addition to their salary. The churches are open and services, weddings, and baptisms are taking place. Many others are working to bring the parks and flower gardens into order. The theater is open, and always full. One has to order tickets two weeks in advance. We don't have this last problem, since the entire Radlovsky Theater is at our place almost every day and we get so many complimentary tickets that we can even give them to our friends.

November 18, 1942   Varja Tumanova, a Leningrader with whom we had become acquainted in Pyatigorsk, has entered the Propaganda Division, writing articles about subjects formerly taboo. She is very satisfied with her work. Until the German seizure of the Caucasus, it was dangerous for a journalist to write about many subjects. Now she is in her element.

November 21, 1942   The one problem still bothering those with even a tangential relationship to it is the Jewish question. A few days ago a neighbor told me that all her Jewish acquaintances, doctors, lawyers, etc., who had some money have long since

*Ground meat baked with a dough cover, meat pies. They are small, like enchiladas.—Ed.

left Pyatigorsk. There were exceptions among them, those who didn't believe in the possibility of their destruction by the Nazis. These—extremely few, by the way—remained. Already, only a few weeks after the Nazi occupation of the city, they disappeared somewhere. Rumors are accumulating that they have been taken away for work. They say that in Germany there is a shortage of labor in the war industries. The Germans admit this themselves. So many have been called into the army that the factories have to be manned with foreign help. One doesn't know what to believe. These last days the rumors about the transportation of people of mixed marriages and children from such marriages have become more and more persistent. Some of Lyalya's friends advise her to take Vera and leave Pyatigorsk before someone reports to the authorities that Vera's father was Jewish. Lyalya is very worried about this. But where to go? She doesn't have anyone in the Ukraine. It's true, Zina had relatives in Kiev, but since the mail hasn't been moving for a long time already, it is not even known whether they are still there or even still alive. At every convenient opportunity she is buying warm things for herself and Verochka.*

November 26, 1942   Today we were invited to a wedding. How nice it was to be present at this solemn service where the church was decorated with flowers and candles and the crowd of guests were brightly dressed. It was as though we were in some different, fairy-tale world. I couldn't even remember the last time I had been at a wedding service, but most likely it was my own, seventeen years earlier. And then everything took place quietly, surreptitiously, in the evening behind closed doors and in semidarkness. We were afraid that we might be seen.

*On November 22, unknown of course to the civilian population in Pyatigorsk, the Soviets had completed the encirclement of the German Sixth Army at Stalingrad.—Ed.

December 1, 1942   Two houses down from Lyalya's apartment there lives a family whose son, Nikolai, has hidden somewhere. Suffering from some kind of paralysis, he was not called to the service. His mother says nothing, but the neighbors maintain that he is a partisan. It seems as though there is an entire band under the command of a Communist who has hidden out by some means or other. This makes us uneasy. If they get the idea to kill some German, even one having no significant position, then the whole region will suffer; the entire male population, whether young or old. Rumors have come of such cases. In one city in the Ukraine, children and old men were shot because the partisans attacked a German officer. Just imagine that my children could become the victims of such a senseless terrorist act!

December 4, 1942   Nina Pospelova, our Leningrader who has been working as a secretary in a German supply unit, informed us today that the situation of the Germans at the front is shaky. Murky rumors are circulating that the Germans are uneasy. Nina's boss, Kleinknecht, has even indicated that he might have to leave for Berlin in the near future and remain there for a while. Nina is worried that she might lose her job. To lose her job with its good rations means that she will go hungry again. For all Leningraders, hunger is the most terrible enemy. The local population reacts somewhat differently because despite the privations, no one has had to endure the starvation that the surrounded Leningraders had to endure.

December 9, 1942   Rumors are coming from all directions, and there is an unclear but growing feeling of anxiety. All of those who have men in the family between sixteen and fifty-five, that is, those who came under the last edict of the Bolsheviks before the withdrawal of the Soviet forces from Pyatigorsk, are preparing to leave for somewhere in the Ukraine, further from the scene of military activity.* Indeed, some of our cities have already changed hands several times, and these were the most frightening times for those who remained. This could also be the case with Pyatigorsk. I have to be just as worried as the others, because in October Dima was sixteen years old. The fact that at the moment of the Red withdrawal he was only fifteen is not much consolation. It's scarcely likely that they will be that exact in their approach to such cases. Most likely of all is that they will shoot everybody whom they come across. However, Lyalya, even though her husband falls into this category, is most worried about her daughter, who will suffer from the Germans if anyone reports her. Under this double threat there is only one way out—to leave Pyatigorsk.

December 11, 1942   They have begun taking people for work in Germany. For the first months it was all done on a volunteer basis, but the number of volunteers was not too large. Now it is forced transport of labor, especially of the young and the unemployed. It is said that entire trains of workers are being sent from the Ukraine and from Rostov. It's true that one doesn't know what to believe; however, since even here the registration has begun, one is inclined to take such reports seriously and not dismiss them as idle fantasy. Some of our acquaintances have already departed. Before leaving, one of my Leningrad friends told us how beautifully her future life in Germany had been described to her—a nice, secure, comfortable life in a small German city, good pay, easy work, and good rations. This woman, one of the evacuees who had endured all the hardships

---

*The Soviet military command issued the order to shoot all men between the ages of sixteen and fifty-five. They wanted the entire civilian population to evacuate so there would be no working force to aid the Germans and so everything could be destroyed. Also, they intended to use the men in their own army for support services.—Ed.

connected with the war and was living in very impoverished circumstances under the occupation, looked on this as a chance to go to paradise. She is forgetting one thing, and that is that Germany is at war and there, though of course nobody is reminding her of it, she could easily again have to undergo all the hardships, including bombings.

December 16, 1942   Many of our German acquaintances have received leaves for the Christmas holidays. To some degree this sounds comforting. This means that at least for the time being there is no threat of military activity in the Caucasus. A large group of Russians often gathers in the café. Over coffee we discuss our future. It seems that everyone has just one wish, that the threat of new bombings, shelling, and famine would end. People have become so tired from these eighteen months of war and deprivation that no other questions are important. They don't even care to discuss what will happen to us if the Germans take Stalingrad and win the war. Even if such a question arises, the answer is extremely hazy: "We will see." No one wishes to try to predict the future in such uncertain times. They want only one thing: an end to the war and the endless anxiety.

December 18, 1942   Yesterday again a few bombs were dropped. Fortunately, there were no casualties, only a few warehouses not far from the station were destroyed. Most likely they were aiming for the rail line. Our grandmother became ill, apparently seriously. The doctor has put her in the hospital.

December 22, 1942   We are thinking of closing the café for the holidays since all the German units are putting on parties with trees and gifts. Of course the officers will greet the holidays among their own. Many have already left for Germany. Tanya and I have decided to put up a Christmas tree in our apartment and invite our Leningrad friends.*

December 25, 1942   There is complete quiet in the city. All the stores, the restaurants, and cafés are closed. Even people are not to be seen. I am sitting in my room in front of the window and admiring Elbrus, which is so easily visible on a clear day. The Caucasus are beautiful. It was not just by chance that the area inspired all our poets. Today we decided to go to Mashuk, the place of Lermontov's duel.†

Yesterday we spent our nicest evening since our arrival. We had the Radlovs, Bolkhovskoi, Samanov, and two interpreters, both of whom were also from Leningrad. One could say that this evening was dedicated to memories of Leningrad. We recalled mainly that which had seemed long since forgotten—not even Leningrad, but Petersburg. Bolkhovskoi recited Agnivtsev.††

Everything was forgotten: the darkness and starvation of the siege, the ruined city filled with corpses. All of us who had gathered in this comfortable little apartment around the elegantly decorated Christmas tree were transported in our thoughts back to the distant, beloved city during the days of its power and glory. My children and Tanya did not know old Petersburg, of course, but the magnificent recitation of Bolkhovskoi and the solemn atmosphere of this Christmas Eve engulfed them too. Everyone quieted down and asked Bol-

*On December 22, 1942, the Soviets began a general counteroffensive in the Caucasus. By this time the German troops in Stalingrad were in a hopeless position as well.—Ed.

†Agnivtsev, Poet of Peterburg, wrote poems that continually glorified that city.—Ed.

††The great Russian poet, Mikhail Lermontov, was killed at age twenty-seven in a duel in the Caucasus near the foothills of Mountain Mashuk.—Ed.

khovskoi to continue. He read almost all of Agnivtsev, especially the poems dedicated to Petersburg. We did not wish to return to the present, to think about the Germans, about the battle for Stalingrad, about our so cloudy future. If only we could stretch out these moments of enjoyment of the past!

December 27, 1942   During the holidays we spent entire days roaming around the outskirts of Pyatigorsk, admiring the beauty of this poetic region. The weather has remained magnificent, warm as in the summer. Today we decided to reopen the café. We sent Ivan and Dima to do the purchasing at the market, and we ourselves began to get everything in order. It wasn't even eight o'clock when Dima came running, all pale and agitated. He told us that the entire WIKADO was loaded up and ready to depart. He had managed to stop one of the officers who was rushing to one of the trucks and asked him what was up. The officer, somewhat embarrassed and not looking Dima in the eye, answered that they were leaving Pyatigorsk. Dima of course didn't receive anything more exact than that. The thought that this was the beginning of the German retreat flashed through all our minds. It was not by chance that one of the officers of the Baltic Germans, a certain Diegel, had pointedly asked us how things were with the purchase of horses and why we were delaying. At that time we hadn't paid any special attention; now, however, we all remembered his words.

Our friends began to come to the café with more and more alarming news. It was already clear to everyone that the Germans were retreating. If not today, then tomorrow the Red Army might occupy the city. Everybody was saying it was best to get out of Pyatigorsk somehow. But how? For a long time there have been no trains for the civilian population; nobody has any automobiles, neither we nor our friends have any horses. That means we can only leave on foot. This is the same dilemma as in August. How far can you go on foot. But we have to leave Pyatigorsk. Varya came running in and announced that she was going to beg the first passing German car to take her at least as far as Rostov. She is in even greater danger than we are, for she was working in the propaganda section and the Communists will never forgive her incendiary articles.

December 31, 1942   All our attempts to find anyone who would agree to take us to Rostov have been unsuccessful. We had chosen Rostov because we have close friends there who might be able to take us in, at least for a little while. Almost everybody whom we knew was already departing hastily from Pyatigorsk. Meeting them by chance on the street, they would try to give the appearance that they don't notice us. Our situation is getting worse. Today Tanya, Dima, Yuri, and I left our apartment because it seemed especially painful to remain alone in the large empty building. Taking a small part of our things, we moved again to Kochura Street, to Lyalya's.

In a few hours it will be New Year's. It seems that this year will be even more gloomy than the one that has just ended.

January 1, 1943   New Year's Eve was crowded with various events. At nine o'clock I put Yuri to bed and lay down on the divan with him for a while, since I wasn't feeling well. My general condition had suffered because of all the agitation of the last few days. A knock resounded on the door and Varya burst into the room, shouting, "The Germans are abandoning the city. There is complete anarchy. If you have any occupation money, burn it. The Reds might come today and it might be dangerous to have that money." Under the influence of Varya's panic, Lyalya was all set to carry out this advice. We all persuaded her not to do this. Each one of us could hide a small sum on his own person. Varya ran out and returned in a few minutes with new disturbing news. Partisans who had been hiding in the forests had returned and were saying with certainty that the Red Army was en route to Pyatigorsk and that we could expect the city to be occupied either today or tomorrow. I was shaking as if in a fever, lying near Yuri, who was asleep. Tanya was crying bitterly about the fate of her pilot, who had often been in our café. He had said that his unit would be the last to leave the city, after having blown up all objects of importance.

Varya's panic infected us all and continued to mount as shooting was heard. Toward midnight there was pounding on our door. Before I opened it, certain that it was Red Army men, I asked, "Who is it?"

"Sulzbach. Open up," was the cheerful answer.

Sulzbach, one of the regular guests at our café, wanted to celebrate the New Year with us. And even the shooting, which had so frightened us, turned out to be a perfectly harmless German custom of welcoming in the new year. We told Sulzbach our worries. Some time back he had given us to understand that his unit would be the last to leave the city, and prior to leaving would have to dismantle and blow up important objects. "Everybody hasn't left Pyatigorsk yet," he consoled us. "You forget that I am still here. All the office rats have left; they're the first ones to leave the sinking ship. I am a front-line officer, and I don't leave my friends in the lurch."

January 2, 1943   Today we gave all our documents to Sulzbach, who had dropped in for a minute. He has arranged for Dima to move into his quarters immediately and begin work as a cook. Dima hasn't the faintest idea of how to cook even a potato. However, Sulzbach wants Dima nearby so that in the event of danger he can send him for us. He told us to come to him early in the morning of January 10.

January 4, 1943   Dima's first day as a cook was a disaster. He cooked a chicken with all its innards—the gallbladder burst and the soup was absolutely inedible. We were sure that Dima's career as a cook had come to an end. It turned out, however, that Sulzbach only laughed and didn't kick him out.

January 5, 1943   Out of boredom from complete inactivity, we have again opened our café. Lyalya doesn't come any longer; neither does Dima. There are a lot of customers. Apparently those inhabitants of Pyatigorsk who remained have decided to get rid of their occupation money, which will of course lose all value with the coming of the Reds. The knowledge that Sulzbach will take us to Rostov has calmed us. The city is empty. Occasionally either a car, a motorcycle, or a group of soldiers goes by. Today I met the Radlovs, Bolkhovskoi, and other actors who were leaving for Rostov in a freight car attached to a military train. Everybody is so panicky about his own fate that no one thinks about getting permission for us. Samanov, Laks' translator, has arranged to ride in a car with the family of the chief engineer of the city administration. If it weren't for Sulzbach, we couldn't even hope to get out of Pyatigorsk. He drove by yesterday, and catching sight of Varya crying, promised to take her. And that's how a person really finds out who his friends and enemies are.

January 9, 1943   We have finally definitely closed the café. The last products have been sold. A few things we simply gave away. The city is emptying out with each day. Many people are simply afraid to leave their houses and walk in the streets; they expect air attacks and artillery fire. Truck columns with soldiers roll through the city. Often women, children, and oldsters are to be seen among the soldiers. Men of various Caucasian nationalities walk in groups with their knapsacks on their backs.

Their families and their property are in the carts. It is as though
the entire district were moving somewhere. Now it is only five
o'clock, but it is completely dark. I returned home a while ago.
The electricity is not working. The small kerosene lamp adds to
the melancholy. The bursts of explosions are heard constantly.
We're waiting any minute for the power station to go up. It's just
around the corner. Now and then someone runs by in the
street, and strange sounds are heard. You don't know whether
it's someone shouting or crying, or whether it's a dog barking.
Our nerves are extremely tense. I persuade Lyalya to leave and
not to lose another minute. I don't have the strength to wait
another four hours till morning, as Sulzbach had told us.

EnRoute from Pyatigorsk to Bendorf

January 12, 1943   We are again on the road, driving in the direction of Krasnodar. We have just stopped for the night in a stanitsa.* It was only with difficulty that we found a place; everything is crowded with those pulling back, German military as well as people from the Caucasus. I'll describe now everything that happened since that memorable evening of the ninth of January. Having written in the last line in my diary that I had no strength left to wait any longer, I proposed that we go immediately to Sulzbach and convince him to allow us to spend the night in his kitchen. My suggestion was accepted with great enthusiasm. Everybody was extremely depressed. There was a sad farewell scene with the grandmother, who after her recent illness was unable and did not wish to go. She was still very weak, and her legs were greatly swollen. We arranged with the neighbor, Olga Aleksandrovna, who agreed to take Grandmother in and care for her. We supplied them with food and material which Lyalya still had. Finally we set out. The city was pitch dark. There wasn't a living soul on the streets. The glare of

---

*A stanitsa is a Cossack settlement, originally established as a frontier defense.—Ed.

fires was visible. In the distance were the rumblings now of explosions, now of artillery fire. We moved quickly in tense silence. Dima, hearing steps on the rear stairs, opened the door and was horror-struck to find out that we had disobeyed the instructions of his commander and were preparing to spend the night there. Sulzbach was not at home; he had left and promised to return toward night. We sat down on the floor and began to wait for whatever would happen. About twelve o'clock Sulzbach appeared at the door. Apparently he was unpleasantly surprised to see such a group in his kitchen. We explained that we couldn't wait at home any longer—it was too difficult. He laughed at our fears, assuring us that there was still no real danger. But this time he was mistaken. Not even an hour had passed when his telephone rang and he received an order to evacuate immediately. Fortunately we were right there and Sulzbach ordered us to get into the car which was in the yard. He took part of our things with him in his car, saying that he would come right behind us. Not half an hour had passed since the telephone conversation, and we were already sitting inside a truck. Only Ivan still could not decide what to do, and first he would rush toward the car, then he would rush back toward the house. Finally some soldiers shouted at him, and like a dog with his tail between his legs, he crawled inside. Three trucks moved out simultaneously and almost immediately moved up to full speed. The familiar streets flashed past, then the suburbs, and soon we were on the highway leading to Mineralnyie Vodyi (Mineral Waters). I remembered the departure from Leningrad the sixth of February, 1942. Almost a year had passed since then, and we were now again en route into the completely unknown. The darkness of night, the roar of the motors, and the distant firing added to the anxious and tense mood. Again, as in the evacuation train from Leningrad, I was pressing Yuri to myself and he, lulled by the rocking of the vehicle, was falling asleep. Everyone else was silent. Varya was sitting near me. She had separated from her sister and her only daughter. Her sister had persuaded her to leave; her work in the Propaganda Division had marked her. Her sister, Svetlana, however, remained with the two girls, her own daughter and Varya's daughter. Svetlana's husband had been killed at the front.

We soon came into an uninterrupted flow of vehicles. We had to go slower. Those who tried to pass were not allowed to, and there was an unending honking, shouting, cursing. There was an atmosphere of panic along this main road; automobiles, horses, people, everyone was rushing forward toward somewhere, and behind them, seeming very near, there was artillery firing. It seemed that they were following right on our heels. Something happened to our truck. The driver drove off onto the side and stopped. Two soldiers, who were with the driver, began to help him. The motor just wouldn't go. The column of vehicles rolled past. Time was passing. An officer left his column, drove up to us, and told the driver something. Finally, through their combined efforts, the motor started and our driver again joined the general stream. We rode two days without stop. Firing was no longer audible and the soldiers decided to rest. We were all extremely tired and felt absolutely exhausted from the constant lurching, lack of sleep and lack of food, and sitting in a crouched position.

January 13, 1943   Yesterday I was so exhausted that I couldn't write any more. Only the soldiers, Lyalya, and her family got space in the izba, * whose owner agreed to take us in. The rest of us had to spend the night in the car. After we had eaten in a nice warm room, Tanya, Varya, the children, and I stretched out in the car; at least it was possible to stretch out after five persons

*An izba is a peasant hut in Russia.—Ed.

The route taken by Elena Skrjabina during the first part of her flight from Pyatigorsk through the Caucasus Mountains.

had left the vehicle. This morning we had an unexpected and pleasant meeting with Sulzbach, whom we had completely lost. He was driving past on the highway and saw our car sitting to the side. He recognized "his property," stopped, and ran over to us, scaring us half out of our wits at first. Lively as always, he told us all his adventures. In Mineral Waters he had encountered the Reds. His car had been blown up; however, he was able to jump onto a passing German tank and save himself. His mood is extremely cheerful. We, however, are downcast—not just about his fine car, but also because of our goods which were in there, especially Lyalya's sewing machine, which we had especially wanted to save.

Now we are all sitting in the izba where our people had spent the night. In half an hour we'll go further.

January 15, 1943, 2 P.M.   We stopped for a few hours in Armavir. What a sad impression! How much Armavir differs today from that city through which we passed in the spring of 1942. At that time it had not been touched by the war at all. Now, however, everywhere there is evidence of destruction. In the city park there is a military cemetery. In it are also German soldiers and officers. I walked for a long time among the graves. Involuntarily I thought about the families of these dead youths, fighting so far from home. Most likely the parents and relatives will never be able to visit their graves. Involuntarily I think also about my family, whose graves are scattered over all of Russia.

I walked through the cemetery and read the names of those interred. The soldiers finished their business earlier than expected and began to rush us so that we would be able to reach the Prochnookopskaya Stanitsa before night. There they were preparing to fix the cars and spend the night. The car was in such bad shape that it was dangerous to go further.

January 18, 1943   In Prochnookopskaya, a Cossack village, we
spent three days in a peasant izba of extremely unpleasant
owners and then we went on. We have now a new traveler in
our car, Mahomet, a military prisoner from Baku, who is
boundlessly grateful and devoted to Sulzbach. He was deathly
afraid that we would not carry out the orders of Sulzbach, who
had left the previous evening, and that we would not take him
with us. Sulzbach had come across Mahomet by sheer chance
in Armavir and taken him to Prochnookopskaya. There he had
entrusted us with bringing him to Krasnodar, where his entire
unit was to reunite and where he had also promised to take us.
Mahomet didn't sleep the entire night and watched the car. He
didn't trust us, thinking that we might leave without him. We
were driving in the direction of Kavkazkaya, but didn't get very
far when the car again gave trouble and we had to stop. We had
to wait for a long time, since no one wanted to tow us. Finally a
passing driver felt sorry for us, stopped, and pulled us as far as
the next settlement, a small railroad village named Karer. Again
we crawled out of the car and walked toward the peasant huts in
the bitter cold. Even in the car we had been sitting crowded
together trying to warm ourselves up. However, when we went
out of the car into the cold wind and loaded up with our
belongings, we froze through and through, and our hands
became numb. My fingers lost all sensation from the cold, but
we still had to carry some things which we didn't wish to leave in
the car parked alongside the road. The path through the field to
the settlement seemed endless. The first izba did not take us in,
saying they were full of people. We went in the other direction,
panting from the icy wind. The fourth izba finally let us in;
soldiers from our transport were already there and the owner
decided it was better not to refuse. I became dizzy and sick, and
they put me on the first bed. Everybody became frightened. My
husband's sister thought I was dying since she couldn't feel any

pulse. However, I fell into a healing sleep right away. A person can endure quite a lot.

The circumstances in our present asylum are extremely uninviting. The entire dwelling has two rooms. In one is the owner's family: husband, wife, and five children. In the other there are nine of us, and six soldiers. Mahomet and one of the soldiers remained to watch the two cars. The one in which we had been riding was smaller, the other huge, and even had a door which could be locked with a key. Ours was completely open, except for a tarpaulin which had been attached on the top. Mahomet, who had expressed the desire to be useful, was given a rifle and took his post. However, freezing in the bitter cold and biting wind, Mahomet soon decided to go into the first, more comfortable car, and by mistake closed the door. He didn't have the key and he couldn't get out. His companion was also sleeping in the car, since he was supposed to relieve Mahomet later. Under such a guard, our car, filled with our things, was left to fate. In the morning when we found out about the night's events and went to check on what had remained of our belongings, we saw that at least half of our things were no longer in the car. It was suspicious that it was our landlord who had told us about Mahomet's being locked in the car, and that he had just happened to have taken a nocturnal walk to the road. I am especially sad about the loss of my warm robe (khalat), which has protected me so well from the wintry blasts on this trip. In the meantime, while we were investigating last night's events and counting up our losses, the soldiers were going after booty. The majority of the inhabitants of Karer have fled before the oncoming Red Army and often were unable to take their property with them because of the absence of transport. In the nearest Sovkhoz* many cattle were left behind.

*This is short for Soviet Khozaistvo, or state farm, as opposed to kollektiv khoz, or collective farm.—Ed.

The manager of the Sovkhoz who had managed it under the Germans was also getting ready to leave. The soldiers explained to him that two cars were stranded en route and that 18 people were without provisions. As a result of their negotiations, the mechanics of the Sovkhoz agreed to fix the trucks and the manager gave up a calf. We laughingly watched the scene, observing how the two soldiers were dragging this balking calf while Dima was hanging desperately onto the tail. This distracted us somewhat, and we forgot about our losses rather quickly.

The Skrjabins, along with thousands of other Russians, retreated with the Germans through these Caucasus Mountains when the Red army recaptured Pyatigorsk.

We can't leave since there is a delay in the repair of the cars. The calf has saved us, but there's too many of us for it to suffice for long. Karer is such a poor settlement that there is absolutely nothing to be obtained here. We observe how our hosts live. They are virtually destitute. The children, for example, don't leave the house all winter, since they have neither clothing nor footwear. The faces of these poor children are pale. Fresh air and food are lacking. Their menu is extremely limited: bread, potatoes, and vegetables, and even these are in very short supply. One had to see their delight when the soldiers gave them some bones and other scraps from the calf. This event brought them for a moment out of their inhospitable, even morose mood. I didn't doubt for one moment that our nocturnal thief was none other than our host, who had left so strangely in the middle of the night. But the sight of his children, who looked more like apparitions than like living beings, reconciled me somewhat to the loss of many precious belongings, even the Leningrad khalat (robe).

The weather is miserable; cold, wind—you can't go out on the street. The hut is dirty, crowded. If only the mechanics can fix this miserable truck! If not, it will be very dangerous for us to get stuck in this hole.

January 20, 1943   Evening. It is still bitterly cold. Today we left Karer early and have now halted in the Cossack stanitsa of Ladozhskaya.

The soldiers assured us that the car was completely repaired; however, we didn't get more than 100 kilometers when something broke down again. We were all hoping to get to Krasnodar, which is still 60 kilometers away, but our expectations were not realized. Ladozhskaya is a large stanitsa, but nonetheless we were lucky to get shelter in a crowded izba. We wanted to cook something for ourselves, for in addition to the calf, the

Sovkhoz in Karer had supplied us with potatoes. However, the hosts refused to make a fire, saying there was no wood. In the hut it is completely dark—there is no kerosene; the children are yowling. With the help of Josef, a soldier devoted to Sulzbach, milk and wood were obtained. Soon a supper was ready, though extremely primitive. I can't understand how we are going to spend the night here. Anything even resembling a bed is out of the question, and indeed there isn't even any straw or hay to spread out on the floor. But there's nothing to be done. What lies ahead is also unknown—maybe it's even worse. We have to adapt to all circumstances.

January 21, 1943   We are in Krasnodar, Varya, Dima, Yuri, and I. Yesterday we had already lain down when some soldiers drove up and burst noisily into the hut. We got up and talked with them. It turned out that they were patrons of our café. They were driving in a small passenger car to Krasnodar. Discovering what miserable circumstances we were in, they offered to take at least several of us to ease Josef's supply problem, in the event the car wouldn't be fixed immediately. Lyalya categorically announced that she would remain with Josef, whom she trusts absolutely. Varya and I decided to go on this new adventure. Our new companions drive like crazy, overtaking all the cars in their path. In a few hours we entered Krasnodar. Varya had a letter addressed to some woman friend of some friends from Pyatigorsk. The soldiers took us to the address, set us out right on the street, and hurriedly drove off to catch up to their unit. Varya went to see this woman and returned in some embarrassment. The woman agreed to take her alone. We talked it over and decided to go to the very first house and ask that they let us in for just one night. It was a fiasco. Passersby stopped at the sight of our strange group standing in the middle of the street with all our belongings. Well-wishers gave us advice. At this moment Varya came running back, having gone a second time to that acquaintance, and told us that the woman had softened and agreed to take us for two nights, but no longer. We took our possessions into the apartment. The woman, though nice, made a strange impression; we found out shortly that she had TB. I was horrified for Yuri's sake, but there was nothing we could do.

January 22, 1943 We were awakened by a Soviet air attack. A nearby house was hit by a bomb. Our hostess is in complete panic and forces us all to lie under the beds, where one can suffocate from the dust. She cannot be convinced that neither the bed nor the table is any sure protection; however, we don't argue with her since we don't want to be ejected. In the morning Varya and I went to the Housing Office to find out about the military unit which had brought us out of Pyatigorsk. We could find out nothing. Also, we don't know how we can help those of our group whom we left in Ladozhskaya.

Artillery fire is to be heard here day and night. It seems as though there is firing very close by.

January 23, 1943 We found officers both from Sulzbach's unit and from Varya's propaganda outfit. Our mood improved. Fobke, the commander of the propaganda unit, calmed us, telling us that if we can't go with the unit with which we rode to Ladozhskaya, he would take us to Mariupol, where all their units are to gather. Traeger, an air force captain in Sulzbach's unit, arranged a room for us, and acquainted us with a colonel who is in charge of transport, and both promised not to leave us in so dangerous a place as Krasnodar. It's true that Traeger maintains that the Reds are still very far away, but judging by the artillery fire, I am beginning to doubt the accuracy of his assurances. We moved into the house, next to that of the colonel. Traeger found out that we have no foodstuffs, and today we received a full soldier's dinner. This was an extremely welcome surprise. The black market is flourishing in Krasnodar. The prices are completely unbelievable: butter 800 rubles a kilo, potatoes 80 rubles, carrots 60–70, and so forth. If we are delayed here, my 5,000 rubles will not last long.

January 24, 1943   Every day we implore Traeger to send a car for those we left behind. Today they finally arrived. We were able to find an apartment for them and took Tanya in with us. We even have room for one more.

January 25, 1943   We are again underway. Today we were awakened very early, at five o'clock, and ordered to load up the car right away. That previous evening, the soldier Josef had told Lyalya that he had received the colonel's permission to take us all in one car. Therefore, while they were loading us in, he ordered the driver to go to Lenin Street where Lyalya, her husband, daughter Vera, and Zina were staying. I felt that something was not quite right and that Josef was not really sure of his actions. Nonetheless, we did pick up Lyalya and her family. When we returned to the motor pool there was trouble. Josef had received permission only for the five of us. All hell broke loose. Lyalya and her family were put out. We had no idea of what to do. Lyalya insisted that we get out, too. Part of our things had already gone with the other cars which had been loaded earlier. But the main thing was that there were so many of us that we couldn't begin to hope that anyone would take nine people. However, if we broke up into two groups, it would be easier to get a ride. We tried to prove this to Lyalya, who was stubbornly insisting that we, too, get out. We gave her the address of Fobke in Propaganda, who had promised to take four persons and, in case of necessity, even five. Lyalya didn't want to listen to this. Varya announced that she would not do anything so stupid. Dima and Tanya were crying. Yuri was yelling, out of fear that I would get out and that in the same minute the car would drive away. At this point, the driver, in order to put an end to this difficult scene, stepped on the gas and we rode away. The mood was not very happy. Moreover, Josef had warned us that one stretch of the road was extremely dangerous, since the Reds were nearby and were shelling the road. At the very last minute, almost on the run, Mahomet grabbed onto the car. They did not put him out. He was reading the Koran almost the entire trip, covering his head with a blanket and foretelling our future. Toward evening we stopped at a clean, spacious izba. The head of our expedition now was a young German sergeant who had seemed to us to be very angry when he had shouted at Josef and put our people out. It came out that he was especially angry with Josef for violating the strict German discipline and having sent the car for Lyalya without permission. Apparently, if Josef hadn't acted so independently, everything might have turned out much better and Lyalya's family would have been together with us. For the Germans, discipline is everything. Mahomet, however, is extremely happy that he was taken. He kept repeating one and the same thing between prayers: "If only they will take me with them and not leave me to the Bolsheviks!" Indeed, he is a military prisoner, and he knows full well what happens to prisoners who fall into the hands of "their own people."*

Early in the morning we rode further. The road is very unpleasant. Everywhere there is evidence of bombing and ruins. Human corpses, horses, and smashed cars are right on the road. The sergeant, who is now the driver, was speeding without stopping. Only late in the evening did we finally stop in

*Often these prisoners were executed. Those who were fortunate were sent to Siberia. Solzhenitsyn deals with this somewhat in *Gulag Archipelago*.—Ed.

a small village. The sergeant had mellowed so much that he treated us to tea and cognac; this was just what we needed since we were frozen through and through. For supper we cooked macaroni, of which we had brought a full sack from Krasnodar. This time the landladies were very hospitable and allowed us to cook as we wished. They told us that in former days they had been "dekulakized"* as possessors of two cows, but fortunately for them they had not been sent away. Thus they had not had to endure extreme need. Various other people kept arriving, and before too long the izba filled up beyond capacity.

January 28, 1943   We have stopped again, but this time we traveled quite a distance. If all goes well, we should be in Mariupol tomorrow. Everybody is extremely tense. We did not stop in Rostov. While driving past the fields just before coming to Rostov we noticed masses of smashed artillery pieces, bodies of horses, crippled tanks. Everybody is longing for only one thing: to get past Rostov as quickly as possible. We were delayed in Rostov, since the soldiers were waiting for something or someone. The city has suffered great damage; everywhere there are heaps of rubble of what must have been large and attractive buildings. Finally we drove out of the city. Everybody breathed more easily. Unfortunately, our happiness was short-lived. The soldiers again returned and went off somewhere. One of the drivers, worried about our lack of provisions, gave us some bread. The bread was completely frozen. It couldn't be cut even with a knife. Somehow we managed to cut it into pieces and gnawed on it. We continued to remain in place. The cold was getting more intense. Our spirits were dropping more and more. It became completely dark by the time we finally left

*The Kulaks were the so-called wealthier (individualistic) peasants who were crushed by Stalin. "Dekulakized" is an idiomatic expression meaning that they were "collectivized." Actually many died and others were sent into forced work.—Ed.

These Caucasus residents have gathered to evacuate in advance of the Red army.

Rostov, and after having driven a few more kilometers we again got into a traffic jam, even worse than that by Mineralnyie Vodyi. It was absolutely impossible to move. We stopped. There were continuous shouts of the traffic police; the Fieldgendarmerie were yelling, and the drivers of the endless column of cars became enraged. Our sergeant also shouted. It was getting darker and darker. The bombing of Rostov began: the deafening whistle of the bombs, the roar of the planes, the crashing of smashed buildings. It was a painful picture. We were all silent, our eyes tensely following the diving airplanes. It was depressing not to be able to move further and to get out of this endless line of cars. It seemed certain that the planes would notice the column and drop a few bombs. Then there would be nothing left of the entire transport. Indeed, there was nowhere to hide. And the bombing was growing more intense. The sky was flaming. The explosions were deafening. I asked the driver whether it might not be better to get out of the car and go into the field. His morose answer was to stay seated quietly. Turning my thoughts to God, I squeezed Yuri to me and didn't move. I don't know how much time passed in this tense situation. Then suddenly we felt that the column was moving. But what a terrific shaking. Our huge truck, which Varya had compared to Noah's Ark, would go up and down, almost turn on its side, and rock from side to side. We were all terrified. It seemed as though it would turn over at any second and crush us all. Our wild ride was accompanied by shouts, whistles, and enraged outpourings by our driver. But in spite of all that we moved forward. Rostov was already far behind, and soon the auto column was no longer visible and the firing had grown silent. The sergeant had left the lineup of cars and passed everybody by taking the car across the field covered with snowdrifts. It was amazing how he had succeeded in doing this. In the middle of the night we stopped in a small village, Chaltyr. All the streets were again blocked up, either with trucks or with small cars. The sergeant went to look for quarters. Everything was jammed. Finally he was able to convince the owners of one izba to let at least Yuri and me come in. Dima and Tanya came in right behind us, and the others made themselves more comfortable for the night in the car, thanks to the places made vacant. In the izba, where we had hunched up on the floor, there was not even place for an apple to fall. There were about twenty people in this room besides us. There was not only no chance of sleeping, but none even of dozing off for a while. Those who had come earlier at least were able to stretch out on the floor; we, however, had only a little room by the doors, where we sat the whole night. Only Yuri was able to sleep in my arms. For some reason unknown to us, we spent almost the entire following day in Chaltyr. When all the soldiers sleeping on the floor woke up, it turned out that among them were pilots who had bombed Leningrad. Finding out that we were Leningraders, they couldn't do enough for us.

January 30, 1943   The trip to Mariupol was a real pleasure, helped enormously by the beautiful weather. The snow-covered fields were sparkling in the bright sunlight. There wasn't a cloud in the blue sky. In one village we came across a wedding procession. The horses were all decked out with bells and ribbons. There were songs and laughter. What a joyful greeting!

Part of the way went along the Sea of Azov and through large Cossack villages, a number of which made a very pleasant impression. We entered Mariupol and halted in the center of town. Here our sergeant and the soldiers had to wait for their unit to gather. We left our things in the car and went to the Housing Office to inquire about quarters. There we found out that the WIKADO from Pyatigorsk was also in Mariupol and that its office was only a few minutes away. And indeed there we met both Nussbruch and Laks. We breathed more easily, calmed by the knowledge that these men would help us. We were not disappointed in our confidence, for in about half an hour they had obtained quarters for us.*

January 31, 1943   The idea had occurred to us to make use of our experience, prepare baked goods in our apartment and sell our products to the numerous well-frequented cafés scattered around the city. Just to be sure, we inquired at one café about the possibilities of selling our wares. They assured us that we

---

*On January 30, 1943, the remnants of the German Sixth Army, some 90,000 men, capitulated to the Russians at Stalingrad, releasing large Soviet forces for other action. Two weeks later Rostov, through which Elena Skrjabina had just driven, fell to the advancing Reds.—Ed.

*The second leg of Elena Skrjabina's flight from Pyatigorsk,
the route across southern USSR.*

could easily sell everything we could make, that the demand for such goods was very great.

February 3, 1943   There is a gigantic black market in Mariupol. Everything can be obtained: dairy products, fish, vegetables, chocolate, and even coffee. Of course all of this is sold at unbelievably high prices, and therefore we have to ask a lot for our baked goods. So far we have made two deliveries of our products and the café owners were quite satisfied with them. We have arranged our work so that at five o'clock we all gather together and have dinner at home. After dinner we have guests. One could even think we are living in time of peace.

February 5, 1943   We don't want to go anywhere from Mariupol, where everything is now going so well. Our baked goods are grabbed up as quickly as we prepare them. We have already replaced all the money we spent and even have a supply of food for ourselves. After the Leningrad starvation, the question of food is always my main concern. Today I found out that the propaganda section will be moving back, and they invited me to go with them. This upsets me very much. They are heading for Melitopol, into the unknown. Varya insists that we go with them, pointing out the advantages: we would be enrolled as employees; they need us as workers, and so forth. I, on the other hand, prefer not to be separated from WIKADO and would prefer to ask them to take us with them.

February 7, 1943   The decision was taken out of our hands. Tanya became ill with a temperature of 39° (102° F). The propaganda section is leaving today, and they had promised to come for us; however, we had to refuse because of Tanya.

February 9, 1943   I went to WIKADO and Dr. Laks promised me that they would take us with them. Today we had to leave Mariupol. Again everything happened much more quickly than expected. Yesterday evening Laks and Schwartz came by and with the help of our landlord took our belongings, telling us that we had to be ready for departure early this morning. This time we went not by truck but in a large comfortable bus in which, in addition to the five of us, there were fifteen soldiers. The commanders, Nussbruch and Laks, were supposed to follow us in a small car. The direction was Kirovograd, the former Elizavetograd. I was sitting by the window the whole way, looking out at the snow-covered Ukrainian steppes. Everything was white as far as the horizon. Not a hut, not even a tree was to be seen in this endless snowy expanse. Toward evening we reached Orekhov. The soldiers and officers found quarters in the city; we had to go further out with the drivers to a small house, whose owners took us in with obvious displeasure. The drivers lay down in the kitchen; a wooden bed was set up for us in the only empty room in the house, in the so-called "clean half." If we lie cross-wise there is room for all five of us on this grandiose set-up. Right now everybody is sleeping except me. My head is aching, but I still want to write down today's events.

February 10, 1943   We got up early. It was a magnificent morning. The bright sunlight was reflected with all the colors of the rainbow in the frosty snow which covers the trees of the large orchard. It is so marvelously beautiful that I feel the desire to remain longer in this charming, snow-covered town which I had never even heard of and which now seems to offer that peace we so long for. But the drivers are pressing everybody to get going. We have to reach Dneprodzerzhinsk today. We drove on. Zaporozhye with its famous DNEPROGES* flashed

*DNEPROGES stands for Dniepr Hydroelectric Station, the pride of the first five-year plan.—Ed.

by. We were enthusiastic about the settlement built for the technicians and workers, as the local inhabitants told us when we stopped for dinner. It turns out that here there were foreigners working for the Soviet Union on this structure. We had never yet seen such beautiful, and to all appearances clean and comfortable, houses as here. It's as though we are not in the Soviet Union. This evening we reached Dneprodzerzhinsk, where Varya and I found a huge empty house with electricity and a lavatory. During all our travels this was the first time that we had such a "European comfort." Tomorrow we go further.

February 11, 1943   We are spending the night in a large village named Saksagan. After all the tribulations of today, it is a real pleasure to have quarters in a nice clean room in an izba belonging to the village starosta,* the son of a former priest, by the way. I had already given up hope that we would land anywhere. Soon after we took off this morning our driver lost his way and we drove all around through the roadless fields. The peasants whom we encounter are Ukrainians, for the most part, and the driver, who speaks Russian, understands them very poorly. I got out of the car to try to make sense out of what they were saying, but didn't have much success, either. For them, everything was very near, but when we went in the direction indicated it seemed that the road was endless. Twice we got stuck in snowdrifts and we all got out and managed to dislodge the vehicle; once we had to hitch up some bulls. Thus the day went by, and we were thinking that we would have to spend the night in the fields when somehow or other we finally found our way.

February 13, 1943   Yesterday we left Saksagan, and only the first

*This is a village elder, almost like a mayor.—Ed.

part of the trip was difficult. There were absolutely no real roads, but after a couple of hours we came onto the good highway going from Krivoi Rog and driving became easy. At the place where the path joined the highway we waited some time for the car which was following us. Although everything is still covered with snow, somehow there is a feeling that spring is beginning. The sun is warming everything more now. We went into the neighboring woods and there high above the tops of the trees we saw the wings of a plane, sparkling in the sun. The sight of this plane somehow took the pleasure out of looking at this beautiful landscape and reminded us of the war. We arrived in Krivoi Rog very close to evening. The small houses of the outskirts flashed by. In the center of town we drove up to the barracks. The soldiers went to find out where they should stay. They were informed that there were no quarters available and they would have to stay in these barracks. We, of course, could not. We got out. It was already evening and dark. What were we to do? Where were we to go? Leaving our things in the car, we went with one of the soldiers to see if we could find any of our acquaintances in the officers' or soldiers' clubs. We had just entered the so-called officers' club when we were surrounded by a whole group of friends from Pyatigorsk. Everybody was amazed at how we had come here. Among others I noticed Werner and Stahl. They found quarters for us right away.

February 14, 1943   Today we went to the housing administration and there we received five addresses from which we could choose. We took the first and reserved two for Laks and Nussbruch.

February 16, 1943   In Kirovograd there are no free markets. Here the civil administration is in firm control and has forbidden them. It is impossible to buy food on the open market. Everything is sold only against ration coupons. We received ration coupons for ten days.

February 17, 1943   Today Laks and Nussbruch finally arrived. They met Dima en route and came straight to us. Except for a single bed, our room is absolutely empty. The landlady relented a bit and gave us a table and two chairs. This room had been empty and unheated for a long time. When we made a fire in the stove, the walls became very damp, and by the time the room was warm we had the feeling that we were in a steam bath. We have no desire to remain in Kirovograd. There is nothing to do here. There is no food to be obtained in the open market, and the rations are too small.

February 18, 1943   The WIKADO intend to move to a village about four versts* from Kirovograd. They are supposed to remain there and have promised to take us with them. We are very pleased. For when the WIKADO is near we don't have to worry that we'll starve; and the prospect of spending the summer in a pretty, well-situated village is appealing. And who knows, maybe the war will be over in the fall and then we can go home. The future is so uncertain.

February 20, 1943   Again a change. The WIKADO has to move further. We became acquainted with the commander, a Colonel Keserling. He gave Laks instructions to take us with them. We rode to Uman and in the morning went further. The trip was awful; mud, slime, a terrible road. The villages look so bad that Laks decided not to stop for the night in any of them. He got out of the car in several towns, but each time came back

*This is a common Russian term for measuring distance. It is about one kilometer.—Ed.

disappointed and disgusted. The huts everywhere were jammed. People and animals lived in one room; the air was revolting. This is a horrible land of devastation and misery.

We rode on to Rumania. Finally we stopped for the night in a large, clean village. Laks went with one of the soldiers to look for quarters and found a huge room in a German farm. It was clean. There were seven straw mattresses on the floor. We liked this village so much that we wanted to stay there and not move on at all. We went to the local authorities, but found out that without the permission of the Rumanian authorities it was impossible. In the morning we were treated to a wonderful breakfast, coffee, honey, butter. It's simply unbelievable. Again we have to go on.

February 23, 1943   Two more days of travel. We spent the night in Vinnitsa. Only with great difficulty did we get lodging in the apartment of an engineer, whose wife absolutely did not want to admit anyone. No wonder. We haven't seen such a beautifully furnished apartment in a long time—carpets, sofas, pictures, comfortable beds. The next day Laks announced that he had succeeded in arranging for WIKADO to stay for a long time in Brailov, forty versts from Vinnitsa. We are elated that we too will go there. On the evening of the second day we all squeezed into a small car and the driver took us there at tremendous speed. Melting snow was flying from under the wheels; there were woods all around the small, unfamiliar villages which flashed by. There were oak trees along both sides of the road, a solid path from Vinnitsa to Brailov. It seemed like a fairy tale, as though we were flying into the unknown distance.*

February 24, 1943   Brailov makes a sad impression. Formerly this

---

*On the south Russian front, starting on February 22, 1943, the Germans began a counteroffensive in the Kharkov region.—Ed.

small city was inhabited almost entirely by Jews. But when the Germans came they were all transported, except for a few craftsmen such as tailors, shoemakers, locksmiths, etc. Many of the houses are destroyed. In the center of the town one can scarcely find ten undamaged buildings. Only on the outskirts are the houses of the non-Jewish population intact. We were quartered in a large, clean peasant house intended for the commander. This morning I made my first grocery purchases. I was able to obtain flour, butter, and sugar without difficulty. The local city commander, a Ukrainian, is in charge here.

February 27, 1943   One year ago today Mother died in Cherepovets. I went to an old cloister where regular services are held. After the end of the service, on the way home, I met Laks, Varya, and Tanya. They are at a loss as to what to do. They had just learned that the commander was coming today and that we had to move immediately. Laks and Schultz had looked around quite a bit but hadn't found anything acceptable. I joined them and we then went slowly through the destroyed section of town. One izba right on the river bordering with Rumania seemed better than the others. The woman of the house readied one small room for us and prepared to move into the other half of the house, which was presently uninhabited. We looked at that section too, and were pleased to note that it consisted of two rooms and a kitchen—just what we needed. The rooms were cold, but we could undoubtedly warm them up from the kitchen as soon as we made a fire in the stove. Everything was spacious, bright, and in front of the windows there were birch trees. What better could one hope for? We reached an agreement with the woman for us to take these rooms. A new stage in our vagabond life seems to have begun.

March 1, 1943   Brailov is not such a bad place. Here there is a sugar factory, so that we receive as much sugar as we want. There is also a dairy, which supplies us with milk and butter, and a large egg-supply station. In the cooperative one can obtain for special coupons flour, grain, and other things. No one can explain to us why all these gifts of the universe are here. But no matter; the important thing is that we have what we need to eat.

March 5, 1943   Dima has been hired as a translator in the cooperative. There is little work here, but I in no way like him to have that type of work. All his co-workers resemble Gogol characters. You go into the office, and it's as though you were in a theater watching "The Overcoat." It's amazing that there really are such characters—and how did they ever get them all here? Dima's boss, a 25-year-old man, distinguishes himself from these odd fellows. However, he can't stand the sight of an empty glass, and I'm afraid he'll induce Dima to drink. They spend entire days in aimless prattle, a very bad atmosphere for a sixteen-year-old boy. I want to wait a bit and then find something else for him to do in case we remain here.

March 8, 1943   None of us has anything definite to do. My only job is to obtain food, and Tanya prepares dinner. Varya, having absolutely nothing to do, has been writing poetry. She is constantly writing poems, some of them not bad at all. I am the main admirer of her talent. Yuri has grown spoiled here; he goes out in the morning and causes me great concern. Sometimes we have to spend hours tracking him down. He is constantly on the river bank with a host of Ukrainian boys from Brailov and the surrounding villages. Of course he is bored in our two rooms where I have neither any games nor books for him. It's a shame about all those nice books Dima had bought in Pyatigorsk. The school is closed. It's clear that we cannot remain here in Brailov. Varya suggests that we move to Odessa, where her uncle lives. Odessa is in Rumanian hands. We're right on the border now, and there is a Rumanian kommandant here; maybe we can try to get a pass to Odessa from him.

March 11, 1943   Our hosts told us that in the past there was a large old estate in Brailov. The owners of it had left for abroad way back at the beginning of the Revolution. Now from the estate there remains only an imposing fence (had it been wooden, it would long since have been burned) and a shady, neglected orchard. A huge clump of weeds is growing now where the house had formerly stood. I like to stroll through this park and try to imagine what it might have been like here a quarter of a century ago, who was living here and where they might be now.

In the center of the city, in addition to the cloister, there are several churches, including a Catholic one. In the cemetery one is struck by the unusually high crosses on the graves. Judging from the inscriptions, these are all Polish graves. Just behind the place are fields and meadows; in the distance is a woods. The river on which we live separates Brailov from Rumania. At first glance everything appears so beautiful and poetical in this little-known corner of Russia. In reality, however, a deep tragedy is hidden from the outward appearance. Brailov belonged to that pale* where the Jewish population had lived for centuries, not having access to the central regions. The Germans treated these people in a bestial manner, eliminating the larger part of the population and leaving only craftsmen whom they needed. During the first days of our arrival everything seemed peaceful; it was only from the local

---

*When the old Muscovite state expanded to the west and to the south, particularly in the eighteenth century, it occupied territories containing large concentrations of Jewish inhabitants. These new Jewish subjects were confined by law pretty much to these areas, called the pale, or in Russian, *Ocedlost*.—Ed.

inhabitants that we learned of the events which had taken place here.

A German kommandant by the name of Graf is at the head of the administration here. Till now we had considered this fellow, who rules this area with a handful of Ukrainian subordinates, a rather harmless man. Now we have seen with our own eyes that Graf and his assistants are not the happy-go-lucky fellows we had thought. We had gone in the evening to the kommandatura to request a few pieces of furniture. Going down the corridor, we noticed some people standing in line waiting their turn to appear before the local tsar. The police guarding these people were quite displeased with our unexpected visit, but nonetheless allowed us to enter without having to wait our turn. Graf was anxious about something and, contrary to his custom, was not very nice. Not having obtained what we wanted, we quickly left his office, but slowed down in the corridor adjacent to it when we noticed the people waiting on the floor and in chairs. These were Jews, and we suspected that they were in great danger. At the same moment Graf called the police who were watching them into his office. Thus we were able to exchange a few quick words with them. We discovered that the entire family had been captured in an attempt to flee across the border into Rumania, where Jews were not persecuted. Knowing that their only possibility of salvation was if they had a needed trade, we whispered hastily to the eldest member of the family that he should emphasize that background. At that moment the door to the office opened and the policeman, who had been talking about something or other with Graf, summoned those waiting. There was nothing else for us to do but leave. On the way, we decided to stop in to see Miner, the commander of the WIKADO who had been appointed to replace Keserling in that post, and tell him about what we had just seen. Miner listened to us attentively and with sympathy, but he told us that they as a supply unit had absolutely no influence on the activity of the kommandant insofar as it didn't directly concern German troops. We left for home in a somber mood, sensing what would happen.

March 14, 1943   A half hour ago, Graf and two of his "police" went past our window, along with that Jewish family which we had met at the kommandatura. They went across the bridge and disappeared in a small woods on the other shore. In a short while we heard a few shots. The shots resounded from the ravine in which we often went for walks. Then everything grew quiet. We sat in silence, not looking at each other. In a few minutes Graf returned, accompanied by these two policemen.

March 16, 1943   Spring is well underway. Everywhere noisy streams are rushing, the sun is shining warmly. The snow has almost completely melted. In the evening, the moon's rays are so beautiful that we don't even want to go indoors. But one cannot live by nature alone. Again an uneasy question is growing for us: what will we do when WIKADO leaves Brailov? And such rumors are becoming more and more persistent. The first WIKADO who will move out are the young ones, who will be sent to the front, and then all the others, since, according to the rumor, the Germans will again move east with the coming of warm weather. What should we do? This question is gnawing at me more and more. There are some advantages to remaining in Brailov. Dima receives a regular ration at his work, plus all sorts of other privileges. If he wants to, he can even get some land for a garden. It is even possible to raise a pig and a cow. At any rate, there is no danger of starving to death. Dima is very enthusiastic about the prospects and doesn't want to leave here for anything. Varya is very moody. There are days when she paints all sorts of charming pictures of the future: our cow gives twenty liters of milk a day and we can sell butter and milk very easily; our pig is so large it is almost bursting, our hens are laying a full complement of eggs—and we are in the middle of the picture, getting richer not only from day to day but from hour to hour. However, when Varya gets one of those Slavic depressions, this rosy future becomes completely covered with darkness. Suddenly the cow stops giving any milk and strikes out either with her hoofs or her tail when we try to milk her; the hens and the pig die from a disease. Drought or torrential rains destroy the vegetables in the garden. Our high spirits sink to nothing in the face of such prognostications. Only Dima attempts to protest, calling her ideas fantasies and her forecasts nonsense. For Dima the only sensible solution is to stay here in this nook which has been spared the ravages of war—a solution which in time would allow us all to return to Leningrad and to his father.

April 6, 1943   Today I was in the hospital in Zhmerinka. I haven't felt well for some time and yesterday I went to bed. My illness brought on great confusion at home. We had to decide immediately whether to leave or remain in Brailov. I no longer wanted to think about anything. It was only with the greatest difficulty that I managed to get into the hospital. Zhmerinka is only ten versts from Brailov, in territory occupied by the Rumanians. The Rumanian kommandant did not wish to give me a pass and demanded that I be taken to Vinnitsa, forty versts away, in a region occupied by the Germans. I had a temperature of 40 degrees (105 degrees F) and at times was even losing consciousness. Miltenberg, a German officer who had taken on himself the duty of getting me to a hospital, was swearing desperately at the Rumanian, which made the situation still worse. As a result I did not receive the pass. Nonetheless, Miltenberg took me to Rumanian territory by another route. When we arrived at the hospital, the personnel didn't know what to do with me. A chance coincidence saved me: the chief doctor was a Leningrader. He accepted complete responsibility. Now it is evening. Miltenberg, having bored me to tears, has left. As often happens in life, he tried in every way to help me, and almost everything he did went wrong. In the hospital there is complete silence. I have been put in a small, separate room, with windows facing out into the garden. There is no electricity. The tiny lamp which is burning makes it seem even more gloomy. I am afraid to think what else will happen. There is one consolation: I am in the hands of an experienced doctor, and the fact that he is from my Leningrad means a great deal to me.

April 10, 1943   This is when I feel loneliness especially sharply. Formerly when I would get ill in Leningrad, I was the center of general attention. Not only my own family, but also my friends would surround me with care and attention and visit me constantly. My husband would get the best doctors. It was even pleasant to relax in such an atmosphere. Now, however, everything is different. Since I have come to Zhmerinka there is no hope that either Tanya or Varya or Dima will come and bring Yuri, whom I especially miss. I feel completely cut off from the rest of the world. My mood is bolstered somewhat by a good relationship with the personnel and especially the chief doctor. The latter visits me several times a day and assures me that I shall soon be well. I can't free myself of the fear that the WIKADO will leave and that we'll get stuck in Brailov. The more I think about this, the more I become convinced that we cannot remain here long. Indeed, with the departure of WIKADO we'll be in the power of Graf and his kind.

April 15, 1943   There is great joy today. One of the WIKADO officers, Schreiner, obtained permission to visit me and brought Yuri with him. Thanks to Tanya's attentions and efforts, my absence has not made any impression on him. He is wearing my favorite sailor suit and looks happy and healthy. He is full of hopes for future adventures, that is, of leaving with the WIKADO, which is returning in the direction of Krivoi Rog. Excitedly I questioned Schreiner. Indeed, the hope arises of being a bit closer to home if WIKADO agrees to take us again.

April 17, 1943   This morning I left the hospital. Unfortunately the very sensible Schreiner could not come for me, since he had already been sent to Krivoi Rog. He entrusted this to the nice, but usually unsuccessful, Miltenberg. Fortunately nothing happened this time and we soon arrived home. The entire WIKADO is supposed to go to Krivoi Rog very soon. I am not yet sure whether they will take us. The beautiful natural setting comes to my aid in this troubled time. Everything is green; the birch trees have their leaves, the skies are blue, and at times the sun shines as in summer.

April 18, 1943   Miltenberg advised us to go to the commander, Miner, and ask that we be taken to Krivoi Rog. Milterberg took the initiative and explained our situation to Miner; this Miltenberg has turned out to be a real friend. Miner received me nicely and promised to take us to Krivoi Rog, "and from there you can go to Pyatigorsk by yourself once we have freed it from the Soviet forces," he added. Apparently he believes that the Germans now have the upper hand again and that they will realize their goal, the conquest of Russia.

April 23, 1943   We are again in a train. Yesterday was "Green Thursday," and according to old custom we went to the twelfth evangelical evening mass. The Ukrainian night was intoxicating. The full moon lit up everything around. People with burning candles walked quietly and solemnly, intent on bringing the light safely to their houses. Enchanted by this charming Ukrainian night, we joined the procession. When we arrived home, two officers from WIKADO, Miltenberg and Wolf, were waiting for us. It was unpleasant to be called back to reality. Wolf was simply beside himself, and extremely angry with us when he saw that we had not packed any of our belongings and that we were even hesitant about whether we would go. Our indecisiveness and inactivity must have seemed criminal to the disciplined German. "Apparently with you one has to act decisively," he said. "Tomorrow Mr. Miltenberg will come by about noon and take you and your things."

And that's the way it was. At eleven o'clock our things were already picked up and we went to the paymaster, Ferger, who took us in a small car to the railroad station. There a place was found for us in a freight car which was intended primarily for the baggage and equipment of the WIKADO. But there was still room for us and all our belongings. A certain Keirat came out of the next car and arranged a table for us, spread out our beds, and the railroad car was immediately transformed into something residential, even comfortable.

April 24, 1943   Today is the first day of Easter. The train left Brailov very late. We slept very well and we are now sitting by the open doors of the wagon, enjoying the view of the Ukraine. Everything is in blossom and bathed in sunlight. Our young people are singing songs and dancing folk dances. An uncommon feeling of joy takes hold of one at the sight of this spring holiday, in which not only people participate, but even nature.

April 26, 1943   We are still under way, and I should like to ride like this forever. What is happening now is so unlike our trip from Leningrad, when there was darkness, gloom, and death everywhere. Nor does it at all resemble our flight from the

Caucasus in the bitter January frosts and snowstorms. Now it is spring, the sun shines; but mainly there is hope, hope for something better, for a return first to the Caucasus and then— perhaps to Leningrad. Today the commander invited us to his open platform, where his car is. There it was still more beautiful—one is seized from all directions by the impression of the limitless expanses of the Ukraine, and it is impossible to tear oneself away from all that presents itself to the sight.

Now it is evening. We have just encountered a train at one of the stops; apparently it is a train of soldiers going on leave. Our car inspired an outburst of stormy merriment among its passengers. Tanya jumped out and ran to the kitchen car, which was a few cars from us. The shouting and whistles increased still more.

The soldiers and officers say we will be another three days en route. Who knows what lies ahead?

April 28, 1943   This morning we arrived in Krivoi Rog. While the train was being unloaded, Varya, Keirat, and I went to see what the town looked like. Across from the station there was a large ravine; apparently iron ore had formerly been obtained from there. Behind the ravine there unfolded a very pretty view: red mountains rise very picturesquely on all sides; among the mountains a small river winds, and along the river are oak groves. It is from this that the place gets its name, "Dubovaya Balka," the oak ravine. The unloading did not take long and soon we were able to set out for the settlement. Werner, who was leaving on furlough, let us have his apartment.

April 29, 1943   Dubovaya Balka is virtually a suburb of Krivoi Rog. It is a worker settlement. The small houses are brand new, clean, and each one has a flower and vegetable garden. Everythings seem well cared for; the fruit trees are all planted in nice,

This house in Dubovaya Balka was one of twenty-five "homes" inhabited by Elena Skrjabina and her family during the first year after fleeing besieged Leningrad.

neat rows. It doesn't resemble the Russian villages at all. I had seen villages like these only in photographs in German magazines. Here, just as in the Don basin, foreign specialists had worked on Russian projects and apparently had aided in the construction of such houses. I note here a great lack of greenery; there are none of the large shade trees and the shady woods which are so typical of the beauty of Russia. Somehow this suburb doesn't seem at all Russian to me.

The food problem is quite difficult. The prices on everything are very high. Sugar and salt are lacking. In Brailov we did not have any of these shortages. There is a rumor today that WIKADO is again moving somewhere, to some sort of village a few kilometers from here. That's too bad, because it's more peaceful in back of them. Of course, they can't take us any further; they can't always have us around their necks. Miner had indicated on numerous occasions that we should look for work in Krivoi Rog and stay there till the war ends. It's easy for him to talk. Obviously the Germans have no idea how ridiculously low wages are now in Russia, and that it is absolutely impossible to live on them. A month's wage here in Dubovaya Balka is not enough for one day at the market. And anyone who wishes to shop at the market once a week cannot get by for less than 1000 rubles (25 marks) for a family of four or five persons. The pay is 400–500 rubles a month. By ration cards—that is, at fixed prices—one can get only bread of disgusting quality, with a large mixture of corn flour. This type of bread turns into rock an hour after being baked.

April 30, 1943   I was in the employment office in Krivoi Rog today. There is no unemployment. All of us can get a position right away. Typists, secretaries, and translators are in great demand. The only thing is, however, that if you take a position you are tied down from eight in the morning till five at night, and you can't buy anything for your salary. We have to think of something else. Apparently there is a good opportunity for opening a café; there is not one in the entire town. But we still haven't been able to reach any kind of decision; everything is still unclear. I am dreaming about the Crimea, Varya about Odessa. Tanya doesn't express any desires; she wants only to go back to Leningrad, where she left her five-year-old daughter. The boys, however, are delighted with Dubovaya Balka.

May 5, 1943   The commander of the WIKADO told us to get ready to vacate Werner's apartment, since he was going to return from leave very soon and the co-habitation of German military personnel with a Russian family is, of course, absolutely inadmissible. We are now searching for new quarters. This makes the 25th time we have done so since leaving Leningrad somewhat over a year ago.

May 7, 1943   The mining trust gave us an apartment, but only on the condition that Dima would work as a translator and Tanya as a helper for the general director. Varya was offered a position there as a secretary. I remain home with Yuri, for indeed someone must take care of the house and prepare the meals, which under the present conditions is not easy. The salary they receive is simply a joke. Dima, because of his knowledge of foreign languages, receives the most, 700 rubles a month; Varya 400. Tanya receives still less. Prices in the market are as follows: lard, 500 rubles a pound; butter, between 400 and 500; eggs are 80 rubles a dozen, milk 25 rubles a liter. Meat is virtually impossible to obtain.

May 10, 1943   Life is taking its course, somehow. The most difficult thing for us is getting up so early. Tanya has to leave for work at four in the morning, Dima at five thirty. I wake up when they do and then can't go back to sleep again, so I get up at five o'clock. No matter how early we go to bed, we still want to sleep in the morning. There is one consolation, however, and that is that the spring morning is nicer than anything that can be imagined. Today Schreiner took Yuri and me to Krivoi Rog, where we received rations for five days. The rations consist of 10 kilograms (22 pounds) of corn bread, 250 grams (about half a pound) of cooking oil, and 2.5 kilograms (5.5 pounds) of millet. If we had to live only on these foods, we'd be returning to the conditions in Leningrad.

May 12, 1943   Tanya has quit work. She made a scene with this demanding and terribly stingy German. The German civilians are quite different from the military ones we have been used to during these last nine months. The latter are much more generous and treat the population better. All these civilians who are holding civil positions in the Ukraine are simply hated by the population. Varya is very dissatisfied with her work, which, counting travel to and from work, takes twelve hours a day. Her salary is just sufficient to buy half a liter (half a quart) of milk a day. Half a quart of milk for twelve hours!

May 18, 1943   The weather is fantastic. Spring is in full bloom. Unfortunately, our mood in no way corresponds to the charming nature. For the time being we are living on what is left of the money which we had taken from Pyatigorsk. This will soon be exhausted, and then what will happen? It is impossible to live on the salaries and the local ration. We shall have to undertake something, but we don't know what. All our plans to open a café have gone down the drain. There is no wheat flour available, and we can't bake any pastries from corn meal. We can't get to either the Crimea or the Caucasus because of the absence of transport.

May 22, 1943   Dima's director, Rudrov, has departed, and the new one seems to be very hot-tempered. He gave Dima his dog and ordered him to keep it on a leash at all times. The dog broke away, however, and took off. Tanya, coming back from the market, saw this director shouting at Dima and even reaching for his revolver. We had been told earlier that this cretin had shot his secretary, a Ukrainian. Alarmed by Tanya, I raced over to WIKADO for help. The new commander, Schwartz, received me very warmly and drove off immediately, taking Schreiner and me with him. In the mining administration he gave the director a vicious tongue-lashing, reminding him that partisans were now operating all over the Ukraine and blaming the civil administration for ruining everything that had been achieved by the military units. The director, confused and embarrassed, squirmed helplessly in his chair and couldn't find a thing to say in self-defense. I experienced his humiliation with delight and looked at our defender with gratitude. After this incident the director was extremely nice to Dima, but I am now afraid to have Dima remain at this work, especially if the WIKADO leaves Dubovaya Balka. And there has already been much talk about that. It is now evening, but I was so upset today that I still cannot calm down at all. Yuri is also awake. He and his band of boys had run around for hours trying to help Dima catch his dog. Involuntarily the question arises, from whom and on what does our well-being and even our life depend?

May 24, 1943   It is good that there are also bright spots in life. Today my mood improved 100 percent; everything seems different. What happened was that about two weeks ago, when Miltenberg was leaving for Germany, I had given him an announcement for the Berlin newspaper that I was looking for relatives and friends. Today I received two answers, one from a cousin in Vienna and another from Dresden from Marina Tolbuzina, whom I had thought had been killed long ago in the trenches near Leningrad. It is good to know that she is alive and well and is living with relatives in Dresden. My cousin Sergei, however, wants us to come to Vienna where he is living with the family of his brother, Alexander. Simultaneously with this news I received a letter from Dr. Laks, who wrote that he had arranged for us to work in a factory in Germany, near Koblenz, in a rather small place named Bendorf. My head is spinning from all this news. What to do, and how? Indeed, there are no trains for the civilian population. Even here in the Ukraine it is impossible to move anywhere; how can one even think of getting to Germany or to Austria? At the same time, we basically really don't want to leave because we have had enough of moving around in unfamiliar places. Also, we don't want to get too far from home. The impression is that the Germans are again moving forward. Maybe we will be able to follow them to Pyatigorsk, and then—who knows, maybe we can even get home! The dark days in Leningrad have been forgotten, and we think about that city as home, and as heaven on earth. But everything is so unclear; all these plans can be realized only in our imagination. The most frightening thing would be remaining here in Dubovaya Balka if WIKADO moves on and doesn't take us with them. These civil authorities will not forgive us their humiliation and the intercession of Schwartz and the other military. The second question is of a completely material character. During this last month I have gone through 13,000 rubles. I now have less than 7000. No type of job here will help. Besides a job, there is no other occupation we can think of. I am uneasy, in spite of the good news I have received. I have to think of something to get out of here. It is a good thing that the children are content with their life here in Dubovaya Balka. Dima has been attracted to a seventeen-year-old girl named Tamara and spends all his evenings with her, and Yuri has a host of friends with whom he runs around from morning till night.

June 3, 1943   Schreiner, our main help and defender, has left. How much he did for us! More than anyone else. He saw better than the others our rather difficult situation and aided us in any way he could. Now it will be still more difficult. Varya has been invited by a private firm in Klievatka to manage the casino. This is not bad; at least she will get enough to eat there. The pay, of course, is laughable: some 450 rubles a month!

June 6, 1943   Miltenberg arrived yesterday. He came to see us in the evening and told us absolutely unbelievable things. Olga

Navrotskaya, my cousin whom I had asked him to try to find, thinking that she might be in Germany, is the wife of the German General Consul in Paris, Karl Walter. This surprised and pleased me very much. In the first place, I had always liked Olga; and in the second, this could help decide our fates. For we still haven't the faintest idea of what we should do.

June 10, 1943   Miltenberg has left again, this time on furlough. Life is like a movie film; new people are constantly appearing, play a role in our lives, and then disappear, and maybe we never see them again. Before his departure, Miltenberg brought us a whole lot of things, many of which we hadn't seen for a long time: real soap, shampoo, hair and clothes brushes, an alarm clock, and a thermos jug. He gave Dima a razor in a case and a watch—true, an old round one on a chain, but Dima is over-joyed. Yurochka received a whistle. Miltenberg turned every-one in the house against him with this last gift, for the whistle doesn't stop until Yuri is asleep. Upon leaving, Miltenberg promised to visit Olga in Paris and to speak with her.

June 16, 1943   It has become frightfully hot. Spring in the Ukraine begins in the middle of April. May is beautiful; everything blooms, and it is warm. Now, however, it is real summer. I am debating what I should do. One thing is clear: we cannot stay either in Dubovaya Balka or in Krivoi Rog. Most of all we would like to get to the Crimea and find something there for the time being. However, a family which recently arrived with a military unit from the Crimea told us that people there are simply starving. This is of course what we fear most!

June 17, 1943   We are busy with uniforming Dima. The director of the mining trust issued him a suit for 600 rubles, with payments over a three-month period. He was given boots for temporary use, and we ordered trousers from the material Schreiner had given us. The tailor took three loaves of bread for his work. Dima is dreaming of getting a bicycle. I am afraid this is absolutely unobtainable. Such items are not sold in any stores, and it is impossible to buy a used one from the local inhabitants, for no one wishes to give up such a treasure. In the event that they would be forced to such a step, they would ask such an unbelievable amount of food that we wouldn't be able to manage to pay it. I remember how jealous I was while still in Leningrad when the chief engineer of the factory in which my husband, Sergei, was working gave his daughter, Dima's friend, a bicycle. We couldn't even begin to afford any such thing. At that time a bicycle cost 800 rubles, and Sergei's monthly salary was 1200. A bike was, therefore, an unattainable luxury. Last summer Sergei wrote to Dima in Pyatigorsk that he had succeeded in getting a bicycle for Dima and that he would save it for our return. During the siege and starvation, such things were much easier to get because people were far more interested in food.

Yuri has found himself a girl friend, a neighboring German girl whose father has come here for the working of the ores. The little one often comes to us and when she doesn't want to play with him, he falls into despair and wants to write her a letter of explanation, even though he still can't write in any language, and threatens to shoot himself if she continues to ignore him. Just imagine what passions are developing under the southern sky!

Tanya has given up her job and decided to work at the casino where Varya is.

June 20, 1943   There is no mail from anywhere. It's as though everyone has forgotten us. Even our true and faithful helper, Schreiner, has been silent since he went to Nova-Ukrainka. And also nothing has been heard from Laks.

Dima is overjoyed, for Bennig, his new boss, has ordered a bike for him. He is supposed to get it today from the warehouse in Krivoi Rog. Now he will ride to work and not walk three kilometers there and back. Yesterday a gypsy woman latched onto me and insisted, despite all my protests, on telling my fortune, forecasting for me a long, long journey, only not home.

June 22, 1943   Today is the second anniversary of the outbreak of the German–Soviet war. How clearly I remember this day two years ago. How much we have lived through during this time!

June 26, 1943   Galya, who had helped us with the housekeeping, has just arrived with the announcement that in the nearby villages there is talk about the arrival of Soviet forces. Perhaps this is just the regular propaganda of the pro-Soviet partisans who are dispersed in the villages and are hiding until the moment arrives. This news is disturbing. Nothing is heard about what is happening at the front. Last year the Germans began their attack on June 28. What will happen now?

July 10, 1943   During these last few days events have been occurring which have completely changed our life. On July 6, I was going to the market with Yuri, completely at ease. We hadn't even finished our purchases when I was stopped by a German in a brown uniform, accompanied by another official and a girl translator. Having asked several questions and finding out who and what we were, he announced that Dima, Tanya, and I had been mobilized for work in Germany. He paid absolutely no attention to all my protestations that Dima and Tanya were already working for the Germans here in Dubovaya Balka, saying that mobilization for work in Germany had first priority and that nobody had the right to resist this law, confirmed by the highest German authorities. The only "grace" he showed us was that he took us home in his car and waited for us while we prepared our things to take to the assembly point. Tanya and Dima had returned from work and were already there. We had no opportunity to take leave either from Varya or from Tanya's and Dima's bosses, or the WIKADO, or anyone else. The official told us that he himself would take care of that and that now there was no time to be lost, since the transport to Germany was leaving the next day. There were already many people at the assembly point, mostly young boys and girls ages from sixteen to eighteen. At first it seemed that I was the oldest among all those mobilized, but after a while I noticed a few other women, some of whom were with children. I felt almost paralyzed. Indeed, we had always hoped to be able to return to Pyatigorsk and from there to Leningrad. The officers of the WIKADO had encouraged us in this idea. Now, however, all our plans were shattered. Of course we hadn't the faintest idea of where we were being sent. That very evening we were loaded onto freight cars, and later that night our train left the Krivoi Rog station.

July 13, 1943   We are moving slowly. We remain at some stations for days and longer. Our transport is becoming quite full. There is a rumor that we are heading toward Lodz.

Yesterday evening we couldn't fall asleep for laughter, brought on by the stories of an elderly Kharkov man, who had already been in Litzmandstadt (Lodz) and had decided to share his impressions with those of us who were now leaving the Soviet Union for the first time. At first he related various details of life in German camps located in Poland. The information was extremely useful, but had nothing to do with our later mirth. Indeed, some of the details were extremely discouraging. For example, the shortage of food in all of Germany, the placing of all refugees in distribution centers in huge common halls, where they simply slept on straw because of the absence of that number of beds, the very coarse treatment of them at times by those in authority—none of these were matters apt to raise our spirits. We were even somewhat depressed upon hearing these accounts. But soon our mood was changed completely because of one woman, about forty years old, who began to participate in our conversation. She was the wife of a minister who for some unexplained reason did not make it to this train. This woman, heavily made up and in very extravagant clothing, seemed to be not entirely normal. She began to ask our story-teller the most silly questions, and then with horror announced that she could not spend the night in the same quarters with men, that she would under no circumstances go for the general medical examination, without which no one is allowed into Germany. Our story-teller, somewhat amused by this, stated that without this exam no one can enter Germany, for it serves to determine whether one is Jewish. Our lady's horror knew no limits, and she announced that she would jump out at the first station and wait for her husband. Everything this lady said was so comical that we at first smiled silently and later simply burst out laughing. The whole car was infected by the humor, and the merriment lasted till two o'clock. Only Yuri, lulled by the rocking motion of the train, paid no attention to the noise and slept peacefully.

Now we are about fifteen versts from Kiev. War prisoners were working around the railroad lines. There were about sixty of them. Almost all of them were Mongolian types, wide cheeks, almond eyes. Someone from the car handed out a piece of bread. All the prisoners rushed toward it like hungry animals; two began to fight. From some of the other wagons bread was thrown out. This brought about a real brawl among the prisoners. The guards began to divide these alms among them.

It's odd that there are absolutely no Russians from the European section among these prisoners, but only Asiatics.

The countryside one sees from the train is extremely beautiful. All around there are pines; the air is wonderful. It was not for nothing that TB sanatoria were built around Kiev. One could get better just from the air. Dima has already run out to look over the surroundings and said that right near where we were one could have a good view of the Dniepr and the Lavra, but now there was no time to go there.

July 18, 1943   There is a big delay with our transport. We are still standing in Kiev. When we were approaching the city we were unable to tear our eyes away from the panorama. We went across a bridge which had undergone frequent bombardment but was still intact. On the mountain, drowned in greenery, was the city. Golden crosses of the numerous Kievan churches and the Kievo-Pecherskaya Lavra were shining in the sun. It is difficult to imagine a prettier sight. It is painful to know that you can't leave the train. Nobody knows exactly when it might move on. I should so like to see this old and beautiful city.

July 23, 1943   We have been transferred to other cars. These are French passenger cars and look very nice. They are all comprised of individual compartments; almost everyone has his own bench-bed so that one can stretch out and even sleep rather comfortably. We are fed regularly and receive soup and a cold ration. We are curious as to how the rest of our journey will go. For the time being we are moving very slowly. We left Kiev yesterday and now we are coming into places which are unknown to me.

July 24, 1943   We went through Shepetovka, a rather large settlement on the former Russian-Polish boundary. All around here

During the 1943 retreat from Pyatigorsk, Elena Skrjabina and her family could not have survived without occasional shelter obtained from people like this cottage owner, with whom she is pictured here.

there are magnificent pine forests, but these are all places where partisans are active. En route one encounters railroad settlements, houses surrounded by high, wide fences and even moats, as though they were fortresses. At one station we noticed on an adjacent track a locomotive with two wagons, all damaged. It was explained that this train had departed one hour ahead of us from Kasatino Station where we had been sitting at that time and had run over a mine. Everybody had been killed. It was only by chance that we hadn't gone first. We are riding in the second car from the engine. We are speeding, not stopping at any stations. We are advised not to look out the windows. Everybody has grown silent. One no longer hears conversations and laughter. Our unfortunate minister's wife nonetheless did get off at Kiev. Her picture of the future was such a nightmare that she preferred this way out, having explained it by the possibility of meeting her husband. Our leaders gave her their permission, most likely because they were convinced that she was unbalanced. We believe she did the right thing in asking for this permission, for judging by the state of her nerves, she could not have endured this trip and, moreover, probably would have driven us all crazy.

According to the rumors, only one transport out of five makes it to its original destination.

July 25, 1943   Since yesterday evening we have been standing in Kovel. We have been stopped here because the stretch ahead has been damaged in places by partisans. Although we have again been warned not to look out the window, we cannot resist the temptation to engrave these unusual scenes in our memory. The last stretch before Kovel was especially eerie. At the railroad stations everywhere we saw the muzzles of weapons. The stations are like real fortresses. Here, too, trenches and moats have been dug all around the buildings. There are German soldiers with machine guns and rifles. Trenches are everywhere. Nobody is to be seen on the streets. When you leave such a station, however, the train goes into a forest, and then the feeling of terror grows. Then it seems that a partisan is hiding behind every tree. Yes, the Poles are a proud people; they have resisted foreign oppression for centuries. They have always hated the Russians, and now they are not ready to submit to the Germans.

Evening of that same July 25   We are still standing in Kovel. It's boring to remain in one place, but most difficult of all is the thought of what would happen if the partisans would surround it. Since we have nothing to do, I think about all the possibilities which we have had. We could still have tried to get through to Kiev from Krivoi Rog, even though it would have been quite difficult. According to rumors which have reached us, Lyalya and Verochka, who had succeeded in reaching Krasnodar despite everything, were now in Kiev. We might nonetheless have been able to get there and spend the war in Kiev. Now, however, we have already been enrolled in the German registry, and it is impossible to leave the transport which is taking us further to the west.

July 26, 1943   We have reached Lublin. Thank goodness we have passed through the most dangerous region. Lublin is an interesting Polish city. In the distance there is a stately building, a monastery or possibly a Polish castle. There are many churches in the city, and all the buildings are virtually obscured by the greenery. We are now already in the zone of the General Government* and the partisans are not active here. In the villages which we pass through, we are struck by the impressive churches which we have not seen before. The area reminds us of the Ukraine, a limitless expanse of fields; only the forests here are larger.

July 31, 1943   Radom is the first large really European station. A train arrived. Passengers got out, very well and stylishly dressed. All of us pressed against the windows. It was strange to see such people, who were obviously unmarked by the war: women in elegant dresses, men in perfectly fitting suits. It is as though we had come into a completely different world.

*When the Germans conquered Poland in 1939, they annexed part of the state immediately, part went to the Soviet Union, and a third part was set up under a German administrator and called the "General Government".—Ed.

August 1, 1943   Skarzysko Kamienna. This city makes a good impression of cleanliness and order at the station. There are no signs of war. A huge forest is adjacent to the town.

August 3, 1943   We have arrived in Lodz. The Germans have renamed it Litzmannstadt. It is eight o'clock in the morning. It is pouring, gray, dark and gloomy. Such weather is depressing and affects my disposition, especially when the future is murky. Everything is seen in the darkest light. We are stopped at one of the stations; it is still two kilometers to the main station. When will we get there?

August 6, 1943   There have been so many impressions these last few days that I have to hurry to write them all down before I forget. Upon arrival at the station in Lodz, we stood in line for a long time until the authorities arranged to have us sent to a large place, apparently a school, where a huge room was placed at the disposal of several transports of relocated persons. In this room, just as our neighbor in the train car had said, straw had been placed on the floor; this was intended to serve as beds. In the center stood a row of tables surrounded by chairs. We had scarcely managed to take the places indicated to us when we were all sent to special baths where we were not only supposed to get washed but to give up all our clothes for disinfection. We were warned not to leave any inflammable materials in the pockets. To my horror, I forgot a box of matches, and was already thinking that I would be sent to jail for that, and nothing would remain of my clothing. But, how strange! Everything went by and nobody noticed it. After a thorough washing, disinfection, and medical examination, we went finally to the quarters prepared for us, and at almost the same time bowls of soup were placed on the tables. By every setting there was a portion of bread, butter, and cheese. After dinner, one of the commanders came and explained to us all the existing rules, the "ritual" of our conduct in occupied Poland.

We spent two days in these quarters.

Today we were brought from that huge room to the assembly camp, which was located in a pine woods. In the pine forest there are small houses everywhere, similar to our Leningrad dachas. Apparently well-to-do Poles had spent the summers here in the past. But now we had come here for "rest"—a little bit late, true, but still in season. There are pines and sand, and it is a cool summer day. I am sitting beside the open window, and I simply cannot believe everything that has happened to me. We have crossed all of Russia and are now in Poland, not far from Warsaw. I could never have dreamed anything like this. When could we citizens of the Soviet Union ever have dreamed of going abroad? What we are given here seems to us Soviet citizens a great luxury. They gave the four of us and another family, consisting of a mother and son, two large rooms with a balcony. The food is quite sufficient, 300 grams of bread, three apples, 50 grams of butter, and 100 grams of sausage and marmalade per person. In the afternoon we have dinner, consisting of vegetable soup. There are also stores in which it is possible to buy paper, envelopes, and soap. In the vegetable stores even carrots and cabbage are available. Everything seems to us to be ridiculously cheap, only pennies. This seems so strange to us, as though we are living in some enchanted kingdom. We have long since become unaccustomed to normal purchasing. In Vinnitsa, for example, a writing booklet for my diary costs 500 rubles, and here 80 pfennig. Dima and Yuri cannot believe their eyes and are enjoying the opportunities which are unfolding. Tanya is getting everything in order and making our quarters comfortable. It is amazing just how capable she is, and how she manages to take nothing and make a comfortable and attractive apartment out of it.

August 10, 1943   I have lost count of the number of places we have
lived since our departure from Leningrad. Again we are set up
rather comfortably, but again there are rumors that they are
getting ready to send us somewhere. You always lose something
in these constant moves. I still cannot get used to packing
everything just right. But our attitude toward possessions is no
longer the same. They lose their value and often seem to be
only a burden.

August 21, 1943   I haven't made entries for a long time. Things are
going along pretty much the same. Many of those who came
with us are extremely bored and are uneasy about their future.
In general, I never get bored under any circumstances; that is
probably why I am not depressed here either. Every day is an
exact copy of the preceding day. At six thirty we get up; Dima
goes to get a half liter of milk for Yuri, and I go to the woods to
get some branches for heating breakfast—we cook on a little
oven, for there is neither gas nor electricity. The charm of these
mornings and the pine forest is simply impossible to convey. At
seven thirty is the so-called "Appel" (roll-call), where the camp
leader preaches morals to us, and tries to inspire love and
respect for the "Fuehrer" who has saved us from the Bolsheviks
and presented us with such a wonderful life. After that there are
all sorts of orders for the present day. After "Appel" the women
have to go to the kitchen to clean the vegetables and potatoes.
At 11 o'clock we have dinner, consisting of either vegetable or
potato soup with barley. We receive the cold ration once a
week, and a warm supper is only planned for two or three times
a week, for some reason. It is good that we are not spoiled and
that we still have some reserve rations with which to supplement our menu, or else it would be very hard for the children.
Up till now we haven't had a chance to look over the surroundings and do not know what one can obtain here, and where. We

have a German language lesson from three thirty to five. Upon returning, we drink coffee with bread and marmalade when there is no hot meal. And in the evening before going to sleep, we go out to drink a tasty dark beer. Everybody goes to sleep early in our camp. I have never been in Lodz, but Dima was there with neighbors and says that the people are so well-dressed that we would be ashamed to appear there in our present clothing. Tanya said the heck with what onlookers might think; we should go anyway. Yuri is now registered for school for the semester which begins the first of September. We haven't the faintest idea of where we'll be sent or when. It is said that we'll be distributed according to the needs of various war industries. Some people are able to get positions through friends, and then they are released from the camp upon the presentation of documents showing that they are needed in some industry. We have to try everything in order to get such a demand for our services. Otherwise there is the danger that we shall be separated. I experienced that once when, upon finishing the university in Leningrad, I was ordered to go to one of the schools in Siberia, and the entire family was supposed to remain in Leningrad, where my husband was working. It was only the intercession of Mrs. Kolantyrskaya, a Party member and director of the textile trust, that saved me from such an unpleasant prospect. Now who will be able to help us avoid compulsory transport and separation of our already small family? I am always hoping for some kind of unforeseen event. It is unbearably hot; the pines give off a stupefying odor in the sun.

August 22, 1943   The heat is not going away. After dinner I lay down on my back in the woods, looking at the clear blue sky with transparent white clouds floating across it. I was remembering the summer of 1941 on the shore of the lake in the park at Pushkin. Now, as I had done then, I asked myself what would become of us. More than two years have passed, and we are still under way—one can even say on the endless road—and when will we ever stop? The gloom of complete uncertainty shrouds everything. I think that if anyone two years ago had drawn this picture of our present life, so far from home in a camp in Poland, I would simply not have believed it and considered it pure fantasy. But what is happening to us now is not fantasy but reality. They are saying that soon it will be our turn and we shall be sent to various factories in Germany.

August 24, 1943   Yesterday Tanya and I went to Lodz. The city impressed us with its cleanliness, its streets, magnificent show windows in the stores, and the elegantly dressed public. Everything was just like I had imagined a large European city would be. The store windows made our heads spin with their many fabrics, silks and linens. It is painful when we think that we in the Soviet Union were deprived of all these things for so many years, things which apparently the Poles simply take for granted. In the restaurants and cafés, coffee, ice cream, and beer can be obtained without ration coupons.

On Sunday we had a youth festival in the camp. I was reminded of the *Komsomol* parties in the Soviet Union: a lot of people, everything poorly organized, not even places to sit down. The young ones sang in chorus—all types of patriotic songs. They recited poems praising the Fuehrer and his aides. It was just like with Stalin in the Soviet Union, the same kind of propaganda party, with just one difference: with us it was "Hurrah Stalin," and here it was "Heil Hitler." It made us disgusted and sad, and we quietly slipped out.

August 30, 1943   Now at last someone has visited us in our isolation. Laks came to see us from the military hospital in Warsaw, where he has been for more than a month. Learning from his conversations with us that we are completely uncertain about our future, he promised to write the director of a factory on the Rhine, in a small town called Bendorf. There is a big shortage of labor there, since almost all of the workers have been called into the army. Laks also told us that it was very quiet there, far from the front. There were no bombings, and insofar as work is concerned, it is the same everywhere and Bendorf would be the best solution. Since this is a military factory in Bendorf, I don't believe there will be any objections to our being sent there. It seems possible that this is that fortunate circumstance in our fate for which I have been waiting, and we will sit out the war in this quite peaceful place. Indeed, the war will not last forever.

September 1, 1943   Today I went with Yuri to school, but classes start only tomorrow. Yuri is entering a new stage of life. In the school it is noisy, just like a Soviet school. The majority of the students are refugees who have been taken from Russia. Today we have been ordered to move to a new apartment. They are disinfecting the house because of various illnesses in the camp. It is cold in the new house. There is no stove. The weather has become cold. My throat is sore again.

September 2, 1943   The days, although uneventful, pass with amazing speed. Today all the children were inoculated against diphtheria and scarlet fever. I only hope my Yuri does not get ill. Under present conditions, an illness often means death. Dima has many friends in camp, especially one very nice boy from Kharkov and also a girl named Olga. Apparently Dima is already in love with the latter.

September 6, 1943   Our neighbors have long since left for the Ruhr, where German heavy industry is concentrated. I am very much afraid of this area because I am certain there will be air raids. There is a constant stream of new refugees arriving here. The camp is overflowing, even though many others have moved on.

September 8, 1943   In spite of some deficiencies, I am nonetheless amazed how much better-organized everything is in Germany than in the Soviet Union. Indeed, there are now so many people concentrated in this camp, and nonetheless the rations are given out smoothly. In addition to food, we receive soap, though of rather poor quality, laundry powder, and other essential objects. In Russia these items had been lacking since the very beginning of the war. And even without the war! Even before 1941 it was always a struggle to get sugar, tea, and soap, especially in the provinces. I remember how we used to send packages to the Ukraine in 1933 and 1934. Soap, tea, and sugar were the most desired products. If only we had had such organization, how much easier life would have been in the Soviet Union! Today we took a trip to the little neighboring town of Tuszyn. There is a wonderful Turkish bath there. I could not believe my eyes when I entered the place. Everything was of white marble; there were separate rooms with showers and baths, and even mirrors in every room. In short, they had all conveniences. Even in Leningrad our living conditions were worse; and of course in the rest of Russia there could be absolutely no type of comparison! I remember very well that in Cherepovets we couldn't get into the bath for an entire month because once there was no wood, then there was no water, then for some reason the bath simply wasn't working, and then there were so many people that you simply couldn't get in. And thus it was everywhere in the course of all our travels. Here the people have become so accustomed to cleanliness, order, and all conveniences that they don't even think about them, and we, like savages, stare and are amazed.

September 20, 1943   I haven't written for two weeks. Today Laks
visited us again. He had written the director of the Konkordia
Works right after his last visit, but till now he hasn't received any
answer. Therefore, he is afraid that we could be sent somewhere if the news from Bendorf is delayed much longer. Today
he spoke with the camp leader, who assured him that he would
do what he could to keep us here longer.

Recently in Lodz I saw children coming from school. They
were walking down the street nicely; they seemed healthy and
happy. That is what I had always wished for my own children. It
was simply a pleasure to look at these children, and involuntarily my heart felt heavy.

It's high time that we got out of here. Polish partisans are
fighting the Germans very near Tuszyn. Soviet troops are advancing rapidly. Conditions in the camp have become worse
since it got overcrowded. In these crowded conditions illness
and disease can spread rapidly. Because of the danger of infect-
ing others, some of the children near us who had caught
measles were sent immediately to the hospital. It's pouring rain.
My back has been hurting for a week already, but I can't go to
the doctor. And this is not the time to get ill!

September 30, 1943   The weather is terrible. The roof of the porch
leaks. It poured all night and now everything is covered with
water. We receive so little petroleum that we have to sit by a
little petroleum lamp as we did during the blockade. We are in a
depressed mood.

October 2, 1943   The weather has finally cleared up. The sun is
shining and our spirits are better. I received good news. The
director of Konkordia finally answered Laks and said that he
would be happy to take us on at his factory. He is especially
pleased that I know German and can be of great help in the

camp for East workers, which is right by the factory. Dima and Tanya will have to work on production. We have just informed the camp leader of this and he is apparently very happy with the resolution of this problem. The sooner we can get out of here, the better. Soviet forces are taking one city after another. Poltava and Kremenczuk are already in their hands. Before you look around, the front will be close at hand. The very thought that there can again be airplanes flying over and dropping bombs, and that we will have to listen day and night to the thunder of long-range artillery terrifies us.

October 6, 1943   What I was afraid even to think about has occurred. Yuri has been ill now for three days, and although the illness cannot be diagnosed yet, I am almost certain that he has become infected with measles. He has a bad cough. So far he has no rash. But it is virtually impossible to get a doctor. There are very few of them and they don't want to make private house calls. I have to take him to a hospital; however, this is not allowed without the testimony of a doctor. Thus we have the charmed circle! Now, of course, we have to forget at least temporarily about all our dreams of leaving and of employment on the Rhine. Again we shall have to depend on fate, be it what it may. I had hoped that our relatives in Vienna would have tried to obtain our release from the camp for work in Austria; however, they were apparently frightened by the prospect of our large family, which might be somewhat of a burden to them. As long as Yuri is ill they won't send us anyplace.

October 7, 1943   Yuri is lying in bed with a high temperature. Yesterday evening it was over 100 degrees. He was burning the whole night, moaning, and talking deliriously. What can he have? It is possible that it is measles, but there is no rash. The weather is magnificent, warm as in summer. We are walking around without any coats or sweaters, but nothing brings me happiness. I am awaiting the arrival of Dr. Laks from Warsaw. Now he is my only hope.

October 10, 1943   Yesterday, despite everything, Yuri was taken to the hospital to the section for infectious diseases, since all the signs of measles had been found. He is all covered with a rash. He became ill on the fourth, and the first three days the temperature was not high. But on the sixth of October it rose and held all the following days. Our spirits are very low. There is no light in our room since there is no kerosene. A small candle is burning all the time. Our neighbor, Anna Ivanova, was sitting at Yuri's bedside and telling him tales. Her son, Kolya, is also in the hospital. I was lying on the bed next to Yuri, and the darkest thoughts would not leave me. There was a knock at the door, and a dark figure in a military uniform appeared—Dr. Laks. Thinking that everything had been arranged and that we were all ready to leave, he had come by to go to Germany with us. Too bad. It was a complete disappointment. The next day Laks went to Frankfurt. He was in a big hurry, since there had been large air raids on Frankfurt, and he was very much worried as to what might have happened to his apartment. His family had been evacuated. After Laks' departure our spirits sank even lower. We have been clinging to him as to a straw. Yuri got worse and worse. He was semi-delirious and kept calling me constantly. My nerves finally gave way completely. All night I did not sleep but just kept crying, not even drying my eyes. I took Yuri to the first aid station and there they decided what to do with him further. Who will look after him in the hospital? There has been a huge epidemic, and the hospital is full of children.

October 13, 1943   Yesterday I saw Yuri in the hospital. They have strict rules here that there can be only two visits a week. I don't know what is happening with Yuri at the hospital. The circumstances under which we live deepen the gloom. We spend the entire evenings in our room. A wooden table on a box, a bench to sit on, a double-deck bed, a wretched low washstand, an iron stove in the corner in which we burn coal from morning to night, a small iron lamp or a small petroleum lamp on the table, by which it is impossible to read—this constitutes all of our furniture.

Menshikov* undoubtedly lived better than this when he was in exile in Berezov, not even to mention the Decembrists.†

Yesterday Tanya, who more than anything else dislikes changes and moves, said, "If only they would leave us here; at least we know this place and the work isn't difficult. But who knows where they might send us? And actually we do have all the absolute essentials. . . ." This is how relative everything is. Our miserable quarters and skimpy rations seem perfectly satisfactory to her. Nonetheless, I cannot agree with her that such a life is "paradise."

October 15, 1943   Yesterday I was at the hospital. I was not allowed in to see Yuri, but saw him only through the window. The nurse assures me that he is much better and that his temperature is normal. I gave him a package with some candy and two large apples, which Tanya had received from her boss (she has been working all this time at the canteen). Today is the twelfth day that Yuri has been ill. If only it will pass without complications! There have been outbreaks of scarlet fever and diphtheria in the camp. I should like them to send us somewhere, almost

*Menshikov was Peter the Great's main aide. A few years after Peter's death, he was exiled to Siberia, where he lived in a wood cabin.—Ed.

†The Decembrists were aristocrats who tried an abortive coup in 1825. Five were executed and the rest sent to Siberia.—Ed.

anywhere, away from here. I cannot understand why there is such a delay! They have obviously collected too many people here. Almost every day people are leaving our camp, but with the flow of new arrivals, it still remains jammed.

October 16, 1943   Tomorrow I shall go again to find out how Yuri is. I miss him very much. If only there are no complications, he will return and we will be able to leave this camp. I inquired at the camp commander's office, and he told me that if a military factory requests our services he would discharge us immediately.

October 18, 1943   I am in very low spirits. Yesterday I went to visit Yuri. Tomorrow will make ten days that he has been in the hospital, and I should have been able to take him home. But suddenly it turns out first that his temperature has again begun to rise, and second, that a boy had been brought to the hospital with a very strange and wild disease, infantile paralysis. The boy had been in the hospital only one hour, but just the same, a quarantine has been placed on all the patients and they will not be released for three weeks if it does indeed turn out that this boy, whom they had sent to Lodz for further diagnosis, does have the disease.

October 19, 1943   Yuri still has his temperature. I am afraid that there have been complications or that he will get a bad cold there. There are very few people on night duty, and there are many patients.

November 2, 1943   Today I was at the hospital, and the nurse told me that Yuri again has a fever and that there can be no talk of his being released. I have never had such problems with the children before. I feel absolutely helpless; I have no idea what to do, and I am very despondent.

November 4, 1943   Yesterday in desperation I went to the doctor and told him all about our situation, about the fact that it was essential that I leave. The doctor, considering that this extended high temperature of Yuri's was a result of a nervous condition, since he had no other complications, gave permission to release Yuri to my care. I signed a statement accepting all responsibility and took the boy home. It was a real pleasure to have Yuri home again. He was all excited from happiness and told us about the time he had spent in the hospital, about the children there, about the personnel, etc. In the evening his temperature did not rise, and he fell asleep quietly. In general, he was not at all in as bad shape as I had imagined, and it seems that I had been simply a "crazy mother" who had worried and cried during his stay in the hospital. Today his temperature is again normal. I fully agree with the doctor that Yuri is an extremely nervous child (and is that surprising?!) and that his condition after the measles could be ascribed entirely to nerves. My previous energy has returned and I have decided that no matter what it takes, I am going to get released from this camp. I'll go with Yuri to Bendorf, arrange everything there and return for Tanya and Dima. Of course, there has never been a case in camp where they have let anyone go on leave; however, I have thought up a plan that I should now like to bring to fruition.

November 5, 1943   I remembered that already last summer Miltenberg had found General Consul Karl Walter, and upon arrival in Krivoi Rog had told me and all the officers of the WIKADO that Mr. Walter was married to my cousin Olga. In the fall I wrote this Walter from the camp and received an answer. However, it turned out that Miltenberg had confused everything and that Consul Walter was married to a German and didn't even know Olga. Besides, it wasn't this Walter who had been secretary of the German consulate in Moscow prior to the war and whom I was seeking. Nonetheless, I again wrote this "new" Walter and asked him, since at this time he was General Consul in Paris, about my relatives who were living in Paris. The consul turned out to be a very nice fellow and answered a number of my letters. Now I decided to use his name in order to get out of the camp and arrange our future. Armed with all the letters from Walter, I went to the camp kommandant and explained to him the necessity for my trip to see this consul. The camp commander, not even bothering to open the letters, looked only at the address of the sender; this apparently made such a great impression on him that he immediately gave me permission to leave the camp for one week. Beside myself with delight, I returned home, quickly packed the most essential things and, taking Yuri, left for the station. Dima accompanied us there. The train arrived. It was so crowded that passengers were standing on the platforms in the corridors and even on the buffers. Nonetheless, we somehow managed to squeeze in; however, there was no room whatsoever for even our relatively small amount of luggage. Consequently, we took only a small bag with no change of clothes. We stood in the corridor the whole night. It was very crowded and there was pushing and shoving. We still had a change ahead of us in Breslau. Fortunately we became acquainted with a girl who was going to see her fiancé in Dresden and who promised to help us in Breslau.

November 9, 1943   We arrived in Dresden at twelve o'clock on the seventh. We got on the streetcar, but it was a good thing that I had asked whether we were going in the right direction. The public was interested in us, and one couple even got off the car and took us in the opposite direction, where we had to transfer. It was nice to see such a reaction from complete strangers. Marina lived about ten minutes from the station. She was not at home, for she had not known about our arrival. Her landlady, whom she had told about us earlier, very kindly asked us in and went to phone Marina, who was at her relatives. Marina soon appeared, all excited, and threw herself sobbing around my neck. We hadn't seen each other for over two years. From almost the beginning of the war until July, 1943, I had thought she had been dead.

The three days we spent in Dresden made a very great impression on me. Marina did everything for us. Despite the fact that she had to go to work very early, she still managed to make sandwiches and coffee for us in the morning. In the evening after work she made dinner for all of us and would not even let me help with the dishes. She said that we had suffered so much during these two years that she wanted us to have a real treat. She introduced me to many of her friends, and we were invited everywhere. Yuri, who had recovered completely from his illness, was happy and perky as ever. On a number of occasions he caused me great embarrassment. Once, for example, when spinach was served, he said, "I've never eaten such rubbish." All of my reprimands had scarcely any effect on him. And when I tried to excuse him by saying that he had had too much spinach in the hospital, he said, "I have never had spinach in my mouth." The Germans like vegetables very much and now that it's war and there is very little meat, spinach is served in almost every home.

November 12, 1943   We left Dresden the morning of the tenth. The night before I phoned Dr. Laks and asked him to meet us in Frankfurt. When we arrived he was not on the platform. By chance we bumped into him near a telephone booth where he had just phoned home to find out whether we had arrived. The trains often don't move on schedule, and he had thought that we had missed each other. After supper in a restaurant, we went to his home. His wife and daughter were in the country. His wife's elderly parents were at home. It was a nice apartment, but almost all his things had been taken to a less dangerous place. Yuri and I spent the night in our host's bedroom, which Laks had vacated for us. In the morning we phoned Bendorf and spoke with Samanov. After traveling the Ukraine, he had also ended up in this same factory in Bendorf. Samanov promised to meet us at the station in Koblenz, and Yuri and I left Frankfurt. The train went along the shore of the Rhine. Yuri and I did not leave the windows. Despite the gray, foggy morning, we were struck by the beauty of the Rhine and its shores. We rode past the ruins of old castles, which called to mind old legends about all of these historical places. We admired the mountain Lorelei, the little towns which seemed as though stuck to the rocks, the wide smoothness of the river and its still, green shores. This is where we would now live! We got out at the Koblenz station and saw the engineer, Samanov, coming happily to meet us. Laks' friend, the director of the factory, had had Samanov come to meet us. The trip on the streetcar from Koblenz to Bendorf takes almost an hour. We rode past the camp for Eastern workers where we will have to live and work. There are wooden barracks surrounded by barbed wire fences. Inside, some wretched creatures were walking around; by the gate was the guardbooth. My heart sank at this sight. Samanov, a half-German, lives in freedom and rents a room with a German family. Seeing my mood, he tried to cheer me up, saying that the director who has authority over these Eastern workers is an extremely nice person and will of course try to create the very best possible conditions for us.

Having reserved a small room for ourselves in the center of the town, we left again, accompanied by Samanov, to meet the director of Konkordia, Wefelscheid.

In Bendorf

December 18, 1943   Five weeks have flashed by as though they were one day. There was not a minute to sit calmly and write down everything which has occurred. Everything has been a blur of names, persons, impressions. The interview with Mr. Wefelscheid went well. As so often in recent times, my knowledge of German has been very useful. He was friendly, and he listened to me—and I knew very soon that I could be sure of getting a job in his factory and a roof over my head. Most important of all, however, was that we would be living in a quiet region in a provincial city, which was, by the way, beautifully situated on the banks of the Rhine. Everything has turned out so well that we couldn't hope for anything better.

Now I wanted to see those relatives who had answered my notice in the newspaper—my cousins in Vienna. I found out that to extend my leave from the camp I had to go to the Landesamt (district administrative office). Yuri and I went to Koblenz and saw the official who handled the affairs of foreigners. We received a two-week extension relatively easily. The next day Samanov took us to the station and we headed straight for Vienna. The trip was far from pleasant. All the seats on the train were taken, and we had to sit on our suitcase in the corridor. Several times the air raid sirens began to sound. Only on the following day, the twelfth, did we arrive in Vienna. There we were met very warmly. We had intended to spend only three days in Vienna, but Yuri got ill and we were detained for an entire week. Toward the end of our stay we received a desperate telegram from Dima sent us by way of Marina. He told us that he was being taken into a detachment for fighting the partisans. I phoned Dr. Laks in Frankfurt, asking him for help. He promised to go to Tuszyn personally. I left Vienna with Yuri, who had still not recovered completely. We wrapped him in all types of clothes and shawls, which our relatives had sacrificed for us. The trip back was very unnerving. The whole way I didn't know what had happened to Dima, or whether Dr. Laks had been able to help him. We returned to camp, and were met with great joy by Tanya and Dima, who informed us happily that Dr. Laks had succeeded in getting them to leave Dima in peace. This had been easier since Director Wefelscheid had sent an official declaration stating that we were hired at the military factory Konkordia. Huette. We all have only one desire: to get out of here as quickly as possible. Rumors about the advance of the Red Army are proving true. It can be expected that the line of the front will soon reach us. It seems senseless again to undergo daily bombardment, the roar of airplanes, and the whistle of shells.

We finally obtained the necessary papers, took leave of those who remained in the camp, and went to the station. We got caught up in an incredible pushing and jostling. We were not the only ones who wanted to get out of this dangerous zone. With great difficulty we managed to get on the train, but with only part of our things. Despite all the efforts of Dima's friend, he was unable to give us the basket with food which we had taken along for the trip. The train departed.

At first we headed toward Dresden, where we had to change

trains. We stood in the corridor the whole night. Yuri fell asleep on the suitcase near my legs. I tried to shield him as much as possible from the people crowding us from all sides.

We arrived in Dresden exhausted. Our train for Koblenz, by way of Frankfurt, was leaving that evening. We rested at Marina's several hours. She supplied us with some food for the remainder of the trip. The food question has become quite serious in Dresden. It is impossible to get anything without coupons. But Marina has friends everywhere. A nice, charming German girl, Gisela, runs a little store in the very same building where Marina lives. In the absence of her strict father, she prepared us a small packet of edibles for the journey. This saved us a lot of suffering, for the trip from Dresden to Koblenz was long and there was no place en route where we would have been able to get anything to eat.

While en route from Dresden we found out that Frankfurt was undergoing a tremendous air attack. Trains were no longer running there, and ours was being sent to Aschaffenburg, and from there to Koblenz. We finally arrived late at night in Bendorf. We got out and remained standing on the railroad platform. It was quiet and deserted. Darkness was pressing in from all sides. The blackouts here are almost perfect, as in all German cities. I vaguely remembered how to go from the station to Samanov's house. But I forgot that there were two stations in Bendorf. One of them was virtually right next to his house, while the other was at the opposite end of town, about three kilometers away. We started out. We encountered no one whom we could ask. The city was sleeping. It was one o'clock in the morning. We walked and walked and still did not see the familiar turn. We rested against a high iron fence by a cemetery. I had to admit that I hadn't the faintest idea of where to go. Yuri, tired and hungry from the long trip, began to cry. Dima and Tanya were grumbling that I had not been able to orient

An overall view of the European continent, showing the route taken by Elena Skrjabina from Leningrad to the

Caucasus, from there to Kiev and across central Europe to the Rhine.

myself and had led them God knows where. Fortunately for us, we saw a bike rider who was out late. I stopped him and he pointed out the direction we had to take. At that very moment the air raid sirens went off. In this strange, unfamiliar, deserted town, at night, the wailing siren had a most depressing effect. Not knowing where the bunker was, we continued our trip. Planes were roaring in the skies. Soon the all-clear signal sounded. Bendorf was not the target. In about twenty or twenty-five minutes we reached the house where Samanov was living. It was obscured in darkness like all the others. We rang the bell, and finally an elderly man in a robe appeared. This was the landlord himself. We explained to him who we were and that we would like him to call his tenant, Samanov. The door closed; the owner went away. We waited on the porch. About twenty minutes passed. Finally Samanov himself appeared, but instead of inviting us to come in, he told us to go right away to the factory Konkordia, where quarters had been prepared for us. Our only desire was not to move any further; we wanted to lie down right where we were, even if on the floor, and go to sleep. Very dispiritedly we followed Samanov until finally the factory chimneys rose up ahead of us in the darkness. It was a whole complex of buildings, and to the right of us was a three-story building where we were supposed to live. Samanov went to the kitchen, where movement could already be heard despite the early hour. The factory cook was busy with the preparation of baked goods for Christmas. This sounded so strange to us, that people could still occupy themselves with preparations for the holidays. The cook called us into the dining hall, gave us something to eat, and then showed us to our quarters. In the attic there were two clean rooms with four beds already made. There was the necessary furniture: a table, chairs, a wardrobe, and also a little stove in the corner. Herr Bruchmann, the good-natured fat cook, advised us to lie down and not get up till twelve, at which time he would send someone to wake us up for dinner. We did not make him repeat his offer, and in a few minutes we were already sleeping the sleep of the dead.

We were awakened right at twelve. We got dressed and headed for the dining hall, where we were simply deafened by the hum of hundreds of voices and were confused and embarrassed by all these people who were looking at us. This was the dining hall for the workers of the military factory "Konkordia." Apparently we were a completely unusual phenomenon, and tales about our arrival had already made the rounds.

The dinner was excellent. It's true that meat was lacking, but this deficiency was made up with vegetables. We had still not finished dinner when we were surrounded by girls from the camp in which we were going to work. The girls, because of their excellent services, had been taken from the camp and sent to work in the kitchen, where the work was much easier and the food incomparably better. Now they were allowed to live outside the camp, in the very same building as the kitchen, in that very attic where we had been quartered. The girls expressed their joy at seeing us. They were interrupting each other in their eagerness to tell us about what happened in the camp and how difficult it was to live there. This was especially true because the intermediary between them and the administration was a certain woman of about fifty years, the camp seamstress. Thanks to her ability to ingratiate herself with the administration, she played a very important role in that camp. According to them, she was interested only in pleasing the administration, at the expense of the inmates of the camp. This news saddened me, because I could foresee some very unpleasant complications.

December 22, 1943   By order of Camp Kommandant Reinhardt, we went to the camp yesterday. The impression is depressing. There are six wooden barracks, in five of which live the Eastern workers ("Ostarbeiter"). In the other one is the dining hall and kitchen. In addition, there are special quarters for the guards, a bath, and the doctor's offices. In the latter there are two rooms; one serves as some sort of a hospital in which there are eight relatively clean beds. The barracks in which all the young people live are somber, dark, and not clean. The double-deck bunks are very close to each other; in each barracks there is an iron stove which heats the entire quarters. Usually it is heated to a bright red, and the clothes of the barracks inhabitants are drying around it. The far corners are cold, however, just like outdoors, and frost lies in the cracks. At the entrance, next to the guard quarters, is a small room. This is the camp prison. Here the guilty ones are put on bread and water. The windows are closed by a grill, just like in a real jail. The entire camp is surrounded by barbed wire barriers, and you don't leave without a pass. Reveille is at four o'clock in the morning; the signal is given by the watch. At five o'clock the camp inmates line up outside where they are counted before being sent off to work at the plant. At five o'clock they leave, accompanied by a sentry. The factory is three kilometers distant. They return at four o'clock. I have to begin my work at eight and don't have to be present when the shift is sent off to work at the plant. This is already a large plus. My main obligation until the workers return will be observing, helping keep the camp clean, helping the doctor during the time he receives patients, some office work, and the issue of various wares from the canteen. This canteen is the small camp store, where there are such small items as soap, tooth powder, notebooks, and pencils. Tanya has to sit in a small workshop from morning till four o'clock. This place is separated from the main barracks where the seamstress, Alexandra, lives and works. This is that Alexandra about whom we have heard so many negative things from the girls. She is indeed quite an unpleasant person, though attractive. After

Reinhardt had explained things and shown us everything, he added that no violations of his rules would be tolerated and that he expects a correct and punctual appearance at work; "None of that tardiness which is so Russian," he added with a smirk. "During my absence the guards will watch for that. . . ." Thus it was quite clear that there would be constant supervision. The circumstances which we have come into here are not very pleasant.

Evening, December 24, 1943   Today was full of many extremely pleasant events. In the morning the four of us were sitting in our attic and discussing how we would celebrate the approaching holiday. We had no tree; there was nothing with which we could treat anyone. There were also no friends who might invite us. Everything around us was brimming with the holiday spirit. Through the stairway came the scent of baked goods. We could see decorated trees in the rooms. But while we were still racking our brains trying to think of some way of celebrating, the door opened and Samanov shoved a large tree inside. Our two rooms immediately filled with the scent of Christmas, and everything seemed happier and brighter. We thanked Samanov for his wonderful idea. The question of how to decorate this tree and how to spend this Christmas Eve had still not been solved, of course, but nevertheless our spirits had been greatly lifted by this gesture from our countryman. About four o'clock there was a knock at the door. I opened it and in came Frau Anna Wuergers, the wife of the carpenter in the factory, accompanied by about eight men and women. Each of these people was carrying a small gift for us: a decoration for the tree, a plaything for Yuri from Mr. Wuergers, hand-made, and whole trays of all types of Christmas baked goods. We looked at this, not believing our eyes. They sat with us for a while and then invited us for tomorrow—one for the noon meal, the other for supper. This was the nicest present anyone could have given us.

December 25, 1943   This morning Frau Wuergers came so that we could go together to the Catholic church. Although I am Orthodox, which I tried to explain to her, she insisted I come with her. After the church service we all ate dinner at the Wuergers. I was interested in knowing how she had managed to obtain that much meat. She explained to me that she had saved her meat coupons almost the entire year, having limited herself to purchasing vegetables, macaroni, and such products. Now she could have a real feast with a large roast. I envied such sensible organization, but thought how that would have been impossible with us. We all live as though we don't know what will happen tomorrow. Where would we put anything aside for a whole year? But even in peacetime, of course, our mentality was different from that of the Germans, and that has been the case for a long time. At any rate, on this Christmas Day we thoroughly enjoyed the thriftiness and sensibility of this German hausfrau. At dinner we were at the Schmidts, and there it was just like at the Wuergers: meat dishes, cakes, pastries, and wine.

Tomorrow our first working day in Germany begins.

December 28, 1943   We are gradually getting used to the work in the camp. We get up while it's still dark and creep over to the streetcar stop. It's about a fifteen-minute walk to Konkordia and it's about twenty minutes by streetcar. Dima doesn't begin work till the third, and therefore I can leave Yuri in his care. Tanya is already fed up with her work. From morning to evening she has to mend the worn-out clothes of the camp inmates, under the supervision of the very demanding Alexandra. It is quite true that the latter tries very hard to ingratiate herself with the camp commander, and only approaches him with the "Heil Hitler" greeting. With this she has earned his love and confidence. Sure of her privileged position, she treats all of us as if we're lower down. The young Russian workers living in the camp fear her like fire, knowing that she reports everything to the kommandant. And the latter makes use of the most "uncultured" methods in dealing with those guilty of even the smallest infractions of the rules.

January 2, 1944   Here it is New Year, 1944. Soon we'll have had three years of war. I see the New Year's evening of 1941 as though it were yesterday. About twenty of us had gathered at our friends', the Levitskys'. It was a happy evening with champagne and dancing. Would I ever have been able to imagine back then that in three years the boys and I would be so far from home and everything to which we were accustomed! Instead of our beautiful Leningrad we are living in a small German town somewhere on the Rhine; instead of our apartment on Furstadtskaya Street, we are now living in an attic above the factory kitchen. All around us are unfamiliar people. Although for the most part they are quite nice, they have all kinds of views and interests which are incomprehensible for us. Sometimes it's apparent by the questions they ask us that for them Russia is still a semi-barbarous country where vodka is drunk by the glass and wolves can be encountered practically on the main streets of Leningrad.

Our Russian and Ukrainian youth are all mixed up by everything that has happened to them. Torn away from their homeland at the age of sixteen or seventeen, they found themselves in a foreign country where at first people could look at them behind barbed wire, like wild animals in a zoo or circus. Gradually they have become accustomed to this, and even the relationship of the Germans toward them has changed. Quite a few of the latter express to them their sympathy and good wishes. They have given them presents of clothing, and indeed quite a number of our girls can scarcely be distinguished from the Germans. Fashionable hairdos have now replaced the former braids. They wear elegant, colorful dresses, thin stockings and high-heeled shoes instead of the sandals which one no longer sees. On Sundays or after work our girls work in German households, and instead of money they receive various articles of clothing, which our camp seamstress makes over for them. It is more difficult for our young men to get well clothed, but they, too, get worn jackets and take them to that same Alexandra to make over, paying her for this extra work with all types of hard-come-by food, which they received for their hard work at the local peasants'.

Our "Ostarbeiter" have acquired quite a reputation both at the plant and in this entire area because of the speed and skill with which they do their work. Indeed, they have become essential components of the local labor force. The camp has been here since early 1942, and our youth have been working in the factory since that time. In many respects they have surpassed the numerous other foreigners who are also working in the Konkordia. Every German foreman wants to get as many Russians as possible in his shop. We know all of this from Grewer, a very entertaining German who works here as the camp translator. I work for him as an assistant. His knowledge of the Russian language is very limited. In addition to a number of curse words which he learned as a Russian prisoner during World War I, he knows a few other expressions which he nonetheless pronounces so awkwardly that it is very difficult to understand what he wants to say. Yet he is really a harmless fellow, as our youngsters say, and they have a lot of enjoyment making innocent fun of him. The terror of the camp is the kommandant. Next to his office he has a small room where he sometimes spends the night, since he lives on the other side of the Rhine, a long way from the camp. Mostly he comes through the camp completely unexpectedly, and invariably finds something which is not the way it should be. It seems he is just looking for something about which to get angry. As soon as his loud, guttural voice rings through the camp everything else becomes still. And woe to the one who comes under his heavy hand. He flares up very quickly, but fortunately he is not vindictive and does not hold grudges. First he rages and causes a great commotion, and then he goes into the canteen where Maria, the cook, treats him with some very fine dish which she has prepared especially for him.

The camp inmates are fed poorly. In the morning they receive a portion of bread and in addition the so-called ersatz-coffee; at noon a vegetable soup consisting mostly of turnips, and at seven o'clock also soup. On Sunday there are also a few small pieces of meat in this soup; and for the main dish there are also potatoes with margarine. It is entirely incomprehensible that our people can work so hard under these conditions. What actually keeps them going is the fact that the kommandant lets them out of the camp in the evenings to work for the local peasants, who feed them and give them additional foodstuffs.

Today I went through the barracks to see whether the young men who had gone to work had left everything clean. The washroom and the latrines were in terrible shape. I had to inform the fellow on duty that everything had to be put in order.

Today also the comical German translator shouted from the entrance in his broken Russian, "Sick ones on the doctor!" From almost every barracks the ill ones came pouring, and I was supposed to determine what actually was the matter with them and translate this to the doctor. It is quite difficult to get a sensible answer, for usually it's the same thing: "It's pressing on my chest; I can't breathe right." It's a good thing that Dr.

Renzel, the camp doctor, is a nice fellow. Almost all of those who didn't go to work today were allowed to lie down on the clean cots in the dispensary room and get caught up on their sleep. Renzel let them all off for at least one day.

Shortly before the war when this picture was taken Elena Skrjabina was a graduate student in French language and literature, the mother of two young sons, and the wife of engineer Sergei Skrjabin.

January 5, 1944   I became acquainted with a German woman, an important figure in the *Wirtschaftsamt* (administrative and rationing office). She issues various cards and coupons for food and other articles. This woman, Frau Kickel, is exceptionally nice, good-natured, plump, and pretty. She received me very cordially and supplied me with various cards for supplementary food for the sick camp inmates. I was in wonderful spirits from this success, but coming home I found Dima with a terrible headache. I am very much afraid that the work is too difficult for him. The main thing is that he has to get up at five thirty.

Especially now, in the winter and in the darkness, it is very difficult.

January 6, 1944   The climate here depresses me very much. It in no way resembles the winter to which I had become accustomed in Russia. It is damp, cold, and there is no snow. How different from at home! In the Ukraine it was much colder, but it was dry and sunny and the snow remained all winter. The weather was cheerful and you felt better.

I am writing many letters, but I don't receive answers. In such troubled, anxious times, one keeps expecting some misfortune. Indeed, the bombings do not cease. Thank goodness we don't have any right here, but all large German cities are undergoing air raids. In Leningrad two years ago, the bombings stopped with the coming of the great cold on the fourth of December. But here the Americans and English are even helped by the weather.

January 8, 1944   Yuri is now in his second day in school. He feels wonderful. I wonder how Dima would have reacted if he would have had to go to school in a foreign country when he was as old as Yuri. When I took him to school for the first time in Leningrad, he was sobbing the whole day, despite the fact that both Grandmother and I took turns running to school to comfort him during recesses. Now, even if we wished, we could not allow ourselves such a luxury. Tanya and I took him there, left him, and then went to the camp. In a few hours we heard a ring at the camp gate. Yuri was standing there with three girls. They had brought him here from school, since he still did not know the way very well and doesn't speak German freely enough. In general, he is so independent that I don't foresee any special difficulty with this school life. My days at work are going along quite quickly.

January 10, 1944   Today it is exactly one year since we left Pyatigorsk. How distant our dear Pyatigorsk spa now seems to be from the banks of the Rhine. So much has flashed past during this year! So many new places; so many new people. Our seven-month stay in the Caucasus seems like a dream.

January 13, 1944   Tanya and Dima are not making out too well in their work. Tanya has been transferred from the camp to the plant; and since they didn't know where to put her, she was finally sent to work in the kitchen. Dima maintains that he is carrying heavy loads for entire days, even though he is enrolled as a laboratory employee. I was hoping that he would acquire some sort of specialty in the laboratory, but from carrying heavy loads the only thing he can acquire is, perhaps, a rupture.

January 15, 1944   Yesterday I took a chance and went to the director's secretary, Frau Theby, a very friendly woman who had previously helped us, and told her everything. She reported this to Wefelscheid and everything turned out well. The director summoned the camp commander and spoke with him, and today Tanya was again sent to work in the camp. Perhaps Dima will be freed from work if he will take some commercial courses in Koblenz, where he is longing to go.

January 17, 1944   A huge amount of women's clothing has been brought to the camp. Many of these things are very nice. The camp kommandant set various prices on these items—very low prices, by the way—and ordered me and the camp seamstress to sell these things to the girls. Everything became unbelievably lively and animated. The girls bought happily. They all have been earning money, and since there is nowhere to use it, they had enough to spend. I am liking my work more and more and becoming quite interested in camp life.

January 23, 1944   Today is Sunday. I spent the entire day in camp, because all the camp inmates went to the movies and I had to help in the kitchen. Today there wasn't even a cook there, and dinner was cooked by one of the workmen. In my free time I am writing down the notes I have been making since the first days of the war. Till now they were in chaotic condition and in great disorder, written on various fragments and sheets of paper. Who knows, maybe sometime in the future it will be possible to publish them as a historical document of a most interesting period of time.

January 28, 1944   At work Dima has become acquainted with a sixteen-year-old boy from Luxemburg, Paul, who works in the same lab as Dima does. This boy is here with his family: his father, a doctor, his mother, and two sisters. The Germans sent them here from Luxemburg, regarding them as "dangerous elements." According to Dima, Paul is always happy and cheerful. I hope that he will be able to pull Dima out of his lethargic and indifferent mood. Today they both dropped in after work, and it was simply a pleasure to look at Paul. He is a healthy fellow, and the smile just didn't leave his face. He stayed at our place about two hours and now wants us to meet his family.

Today makes one month since we began working in camp. I have now become completely accustomed to it, although much is difficult for me. For example, it is very difficult to understand people on the telephone when they speak quickly. I am afraid that I will get everything confused, and the kommandant is very demanding.

January 29, 1944   Yesterday while I was writing in my diary, someone came from the kitchen to tell me that the camp commander wanted me to come immediately. In spite of the late hour, I had to ride over to the camp. What had happened was that a Russian boy had bought bread from a Frenchman for fifteen marks. A whole case had been made out of this. They wanted to find the Frenchman who had sold bread for such a price; however, the important thing was to find out from whom the French fellow had obtained bread in order to punish that person for carrying on such speculation. Since it was so late the streetcars had already stopped running, I had to go the three kilometers on foot. Yuri did not wish to stay home and began to cry, asking me to take him with me. Someone from the criminal police was already sitting in the camp when I arrived, and he carried on the interrogation. I was supposed to translate. Naturally, nothing was to be learned from the boy. He couldn't remember the Frenchman—most likely because he didn't want to remember him. He had been happy to receive the loaf of bread, and the question of who had sold it to him was the last thing that interested him. Indeed, the bread ration cannot be sufficient for anyone, and our young fellows are ready to do anything in order not to starve. I left the camp at 10:30 and ran the three kilometers like an insane person. I was so afraid of the empty, dark streets and the possibility of air raid alarms that I was very happy to be back in my attic. It was touching to see Dima and Yuri sleeping in one bed as I had left them, fully dressed. This morning I had to get up very early and stand by the gate of the factory so that Petya, our Russian boy with the bread, would recognize the Frenchman who had sold it to him. He did not recognize anyone, and after we had stood there for more than two hours we were frozen through and through.

January 30, 1944 The Russian saying, "The world is not without good people," is often confirmed here under the most unbelievable and difficult conditions. You unexpectedly meet people who help you, and through their conduct your whole attitude toward life brightens up. One plant cook, Herr

Bruchmann, for example, does us a favor whenever he can. The only thing I can do for him is to give him my tobacco ration which I receive in the camp; and since I don't smoke this is no great sacrifice. He is always supplying us with food, and in such quantity that I can bring sandwiches every day to the hungry workers in the camp. They have arranged a regular order for this food and it is never violated.

The only thing that disturbs us are the air raid alerts, which lately have been coming twice a day and sometimes even at night.

January 31, 1944   There have been very severe air attacks on Frankfurt. I am uneasy about our friend Dr. Laks. Today something unbelievable happened. At first the sirens sounded and planes flew over with a tremendous roar. I looked out the window and froze from fear. Whole squadrons were sailing across the heavens. I began to count and reached a hundred, maybe more, and that was only the first wave! In a few minutes came a second, then a third. Most likely they are all going to Frankfurt or Berlin.

February 12, 1944   Paul's parents invited us to their place for the evening yesterday. They are living in the center of the city in a small, sparsely furnished apartment. However, the entire family is so nice and friendly that one pays absolutely no attention to the circumstances and only wishes to stay as long as possible in their company. The father practices in Bendorf and is extremely busy, since most of the German doctors have been called to service. The mother, a charming woman, is still young. The older daughter, Margaret, is quiet and serious. I was quite taken by Jeanne, the young one, a pretty girl, dark-skinned and black-haired. Jeanne is so full of life and cheerfulness that one forgets all his problems and troubles in her presence. Dima fell in love with her at first sight. I hope that this will save him from the constant gloom in which he is immersed.

February 17, 1944   There have been some disappointments. We went to get our pay, and it turns out that *we* are in debt to the factory! We are charged for our meals and for our quarters, and our salary is so small that when everything is figured up, we owe them. Again I went to the director. Thank goodness that he is not at all like our kommandant and doesn't drive us away but listens attentively and tries to be helpful. He promised to look into the matter thoroughly.

February is miserable. It is cold, damp, and we are constantly freezing. There is no sign of spring.

February 24, 1944   Instead of the awaited spring, we are having winter in its fullest sense—snowdrifts, frost, sun. It reminds me of Russia and is many times better than slush and rain.

February 26, 1944   Something curious has occurred in the camp. One girl is in her eighth month of pregnancy. There is no way of finding out who the father of the child is. She points to one and he denies it and points to another. This second one names a third, and so on without end. At least six fellows are involved in this affair. Today Grewer exploded and called all six for a hearing. I had to be present as an interpreter. I had to look serious when inside I was hurting from laughing at Grewer, who was conducting this interrogation. He called everything by its name; however, with his pronunciation it was made virtually unintelligible. Even the boys were embarrassed at such frankness and could hardly keep from laughing. The result of all these efforts was that nothing was accomplished. I had to type up the famous interrogation first in Russian and then, after Grewer's translation, in German. These artistic productions were then sent to the

criminal police. Grewer and I decided to suggest to the kommandant that he adopt the forthcoming child. I can imagine his reaction!

February 28, 1944   Today we returned from Koblenz in the best of
spirits and immediately we had some unpleasantness. I had left
my purse on the office table while I had run to the seamstress to
boast of my acquisitions. A hundred marks had been taken from
my purse by camp inmates. In former times, in Leningrad, had
I lost such a sum I would have been in despair, but now
everything has changed and I have begun to look at things
differently. For that reason I accepted this loss more or less
calmly, cursing out my compatriots to myself. These are amazing people. They steal all the time, even from their own people.
Every day there is a complaint to the kommandant. One peaceful fellow in the camp has something taken from him every day.
A few days ago they stole his boots. That was just too much and
he complained to the kommandant. I had to serve as translator,
and in the course of the questioning it came out that this was
not the first theft. Bread is taken from him regularly, but he
didn't dare declare it, fearing the vengeance of the thieves.
Others, too, lose something almost every day. An entire band of
thieves has been organized and is just watching to see who
cannot hide or protect his things. Apparently I, too, have become their victim. I am ashamed of my own people.

March 12, 1944   It seems very unlikely that I shall ever again be
together with my husband Sergei and that he can relieve me of
even part of my burden of responsibility. The noose around us
is drawing tighter and tighter. The news from Leningrad is
sadder and sadder. It is still surrounded; the population has
reached a minimum. Famine, illness, bombs, and shelling have
destroyed more than half of its inhabitants. It's scarcely likely

that my husband survived. He was already so exhausted when we left that he could scarcely drag his feet. And it has been two years since then!

March 14, 1944   The weather has again changed sharply. After a few days of spring it is again winter. I have been told that usually spring on the Rhine is very beautiful. Unfortunately, I don't notice it.

The kommandant has left for someplace unknown. He never tells us about his absences; we only find out when he is not there and all the work has to be done by Grewer and me. I could not fall asleep the whole night. There was such an unbelievable noise that I simply could not close my eyes. I keep thinking all the time that something has happened and that I have to jump out of bed and run to the barracks. In actuality, nothing special happened. It was simply the young ones having a good time, and the guards were sleeping. The guards, or "Wachmanyi," as the camp inmates call them, are awfully rough with them; they shout and beat the camp inhabitants. One of them, Toni, a tall, thin fellow, not at all bad looking, is unbelievably mean. He is quite successful with the cook Maria, and she prepares special dishes for him when the kommandant is not around. She brings them to the guard room covered with a towel and looks admiringly at her chosen one while he devours her culinary specialties. She takes all of this from the already poor rations of our people. What can be done? Complain about her to the kommandant? She has already ingratiated herself with him, no less than has Alexandra, and she does everything possible for him when he is in camp. He, of course, thinks that he is the only hero of her life; but revealing Toni's rivalry will also lead to no good. It's better to be quiet about it for the time being.

March 18, 1944   Today I decided to go to Director Wefelscheid and ask him to release Dima from the factory, at least temporarily, so that he can finish school. I had no hope at all of any success. In fact, however, everything was easy and simple. Wefelscheid received me very cordially and ordered that Dima be freed from work. I don't know whether to ascribe all of this to my friendship with Laks, or simply to a good relationship with this nice, intelligent fellow. In any case, this is very fortunate.

March 28, 1944   It's true that we have not had any bombings yet, but nonetheless the planes flying overheard constantly make me uneasy. Almost daily, and especially about evening, the air raid sirens resound as though purposely just at our supper time. The "Wachmanyi" force us all to run to the bunker. From the bunker to the camp is a distance of about one kilometer. The path leading there is narrow. We are stretched out in a whole chain. We have to drag tired Yuri by the hand. Sometimes these squadrons fly over for a whole hour or more. It's painful to think of what will happen to that city where they will drop their supply of bombs.

Apparently spring has finally and definitely come. Everything is blooming. It is so beautiful that one does not want to think about anything difficult, least of all about the war and the death which it brings with it. Today in camp the whole day was spent giving out special clothing to our "Ostarbeiter." There wasn't enough for all; they had sent about a third of what was needed.

March 31, 1944   Today I received two interesting letters: one from Seryezha, Nina Posnanska's husband who was taken captive at the beginning of the war and who is now working as a translator, and the other from von Walther (finally the right one), the friend of my cousin Olga. He is now German consul in Turkey. Seryezha is planning to spend his vacation with us. We have to obtain special permission for him from the police. Such a thing would have been absolutely impossible in Russia, but here, strangely enough, everything is much easier to arrange. I often ask myself why it is so. Indeed, their governmental system is little different from ours; where with us you hear "Hurrah Stalin" everywhere, with them here it is "Heil Hitler." But nevertheless, no matter what you say, there is more freedom here. Maybe this is because we live in a small town and the people of this part of Germany, the Rhineland, are different, happier, and more social, despite the war and all its consequences.

April 1, 1944   All last night there were alarms. Yuri and I were in the camp, but we did not sleep one minute. These huge American and English bombers roared so powerfully that it seemed as though the skies would crumble into pieces, and every minute we were waiting for bombs to come raining down and wipe us from the face of the earth. A few times there were strong jars—I don't know what that meant. Vasya, one of the boys in our camp, came running to us, thinking that we were asleep. We went outside. There is no bomb shelter in our camp, and it is ten minutes' walk to the town shelter, so we remained standing in the yard. A few women and children joined us. The remaining people were sleeping, in spite of the deafening rumble. Indeed, they all have only a few hours of sleep, and after that there is a whole day of fatiguing work.

The night was wonderful; the moon and stars were out. Nature is so peaceful and mighty, and people are busy with one thing: the destruction of their own kind.

April 7, 1944   All the inhabitants of our town are feverishly getting ready for the Easter holiday. But I am most downcast. Involuntarily I am envious of the people around me. We are lacking the most important thing, a large family, our own dwelling, relatives, and friends who will get together for this holiday. Despite everything, we are alone here, foreigners. It is fortunate that at least the children are with me. I try to drive away this bad feeling, since it could be much worse. Moreover, it is always necessary to compare your situation with that of those who are having it much worse—for example, all our Russian young people here in this camp. Indeed, they have no one here, not one related person. Only the fact that they are all young and all in the same situation saves them. They are not even particularly sad and they are looking forward to various entertainments on the holiday.

April 9, 1944 Today is the first day of Easter. Bruchmann, the cook, gave me a huge package with all types of Easter baked goods, and I took half to the camp. I arrived there with Yuri at ten o'clock, and it was impossible to recognize the place. The yard had been swept clean; the barracks had also been straightened up and brought into order; the boys and girls were in their best clothing. They all looked extremely healthy, in spite of the very poor food they have been receiving. Again the reason is the same. They were never very spoiled, and now, when there is enough bread and they are able to earn a little more on the side, they are able to make out all right. This is especially true for the girls. It's a bit different for the young men. The bread ration is not enough for them, and they often begin to steal to supplement it. From time to time they are caught breaking into a basement, stealing ration cards, etc. They are beaten, cursed, and placed behind bars. Nonetheless they are released and it starts again.

In the evening there was dancing in the canteen. Vanya, an excellent accordian player, tirelessly played all the familiar dances and melodies. The young folks had a wonderful time.

April 12, 1944   On the ninth there was dancing and merriment in the camp, and today there are tears. Shura, the nurse, took poison. A girl found her in time; the guards were called and fortunately they were able to save her. Dr. Renzel pumped out her stomach and she recovered almost immediately. They asked me to find out the reason for this action. Her answer was simple: she didn't want to live, since there was nothing good she could hope for. And all this at age 22! I think that there is another reason behind this. She is in love with a young fellow who has found himself a different girl friend, Klava. This Klava is sought after not only in the Russian camp, but also in the French, Belgian, and Italian camps as well. Klava is a first-class worker. The German specialists are loud in their praise of her. In addition, she is pretty, lively, and witty. Shura, on the other hand, is a quiet, modest, thin, unobtrusive girl. There are rumors that she is having trouble with her lungs. How can she compete with this Klava, who is full of life and healthy?

April 17, 1944   Yesterday Dima, Yuri, and I took a trip to Bad Ems. We went there by train and walked halfway back along the Rhine bank. It was very beautiful. Everything is blooming. Now I cannot help but agree with my German acquaintances who say that spring on the Rhine is remarkable. Today I received an extremely nice letter from Consul Walter in Paris. He even sent me a package. It is simply amazing! Indeed, he has absolutely no relationship with the real von Walther. He wrote me the address of the von Walther who had been in Russia before the war and whom I was seeking.

It was also very nice to get a letter from Zubov, an old friend of the family, from Belgium.

April 22, 1944   On the nineteenth actors from Dniepropetrovsk performed in our camp. They have been performing in camps in Germany now for a number of months. They put on a quite entertaining play. The hall was full and everyone was delighted. Our night shift, which had to go to work at four o'clock, was very disappointed. We all implored the kommandant to allow them to remain to see the rest; however, he was adamant.

April 23, 1944   Today I was called from the camp to come to see a certain Herr Roeder from the criminal police. I had to serve as a translator between him and a Frenchman. What had happened was that at work a certain Hollander had accused the Germans of mistreatment of the French population, and a Frenchman working there had supposedly confirmed this, saying that the Germans had even cut off the ears and fingers of French children. Someone reported this conversation to the police. Everybody was called in for a hearing. Fortunately nothing came of it. The Frenchman defended himself; so did the Hollander, and Roeder believed them.

Yesterday was the first air attack on Koblenz. The alarm sirens began at 6 o'clock. We were in the camp and didn't even get to finish our supper, since we were all sent out from the kitchen and the barracks. The planes kept flying over endlessly. We counted 500. We saw flare rockets dropped over Koblenz, and right after that began the hail of bombs on the city. Fires broke out. During this time we were all in the field behind the camp.

At nine o'clock I went with Yuri to the Konkordia. The entire horizon was covered with a red glow.

This morning we found out that about 200 people had been killed in Koblenz. There has been a great deal of destruction. Both incendiary and explosive bombs were dropped. It is said that one third of Koblenz was destroyed. The war has again come right up to us. Will it last long? Will we survive? I keep asking myself these questions, for which there is no certain answer.

April 24, 1944   I don't know where to spend the night. It's eerie and frightening in the Konkordia, and it's no better in the camp. Nowhere is there a safe bomb shelter. There are air raid alarms almost every night. Life now consists of sleepless nights because of the roar of the airplanes, work which is beyond our strength because of the lack of sleep, and a few rare happy moments of admiration of nature, which is now reaching its full spring development. Everything is white from the flowering apple, cherry, and other fruit trees. Beyond this cover is the silvery Rhine, and further, on the other bank, are green meadows and fields. I believe that I have never in my life seen such beauty. But all of this immediately seems to disappear when the air raid sirens start sounding and right after that there resounds the deafening roar of the planes. Sometimes the alarm lasts almost the entire night, and in the morning you go to work swaying from fatigue. You still have to work the whole day, which requires concentration, even though your only wish is to throw yourself onto a bed and sleep, sleep, sleep.

May 5, 1944   Young men are beginning to flee from the camp. At first three ran away, one of whom was the hero of our famous Klava. Learning of his departure, she lay down in bed and didn't go to work, in spite of the shouts of the "Wachmanyi," who wanted to drive her out. During the day her condition worsened so much that she was half-dragged to the dispensary. Doctor Renzel suspected that she had taken poison, following the example of Shura. However, it is apparently just some kind of nervous shock, which is rather rare for someone so young, healthy, and strong.

A few days later two more lads ran away, having previously written the kommandant an anonymous letter stating that if they weren't given all types of privileges, permission to walk around till 10 o'clock in the evening, permission to bring to camp all the foodstuffs they received from the peasants, and an increase in the bread ration, then by the end of the month thirty more fellows would flee. The first three who ran away on May first have not been found.

May 13, 1944   Today is Yuri's birthday. Instead of a holiday spirit, there is only gloom. Last night I was not able to sleep more than three hours, and of course I am simply beat today. If it continues this way, then our health will not hold up. The Anglo-American bombings are worse than those of the Germans which we experienced in Leningrad. The latter, with German punctuality, would fly over daily at seven and very seldom would they come later. They never came at night, and thus one could always rest. But the Allies fly without any type of schedule, whenever they feel like it, and they roar overhead all night. This has been going on since December; however, we used to think that Bendorf could not possibly be the target of their attention, and we were able to ignore them and sleep.

May 14, 1944   Since last night was quiet with no alarms, and we had a good night's sleep, we are celebrating Yuri's birthday today. Dima touched me very much because he searched out in Koblenz such nice toys for Yuri. These were toys beyond the wildest dreams of anything Yuri could have imagined. He was especially pleased with a wind-up airplane and toy soldiers.

Today there was a big event in the camp. Grewer drove to Cologne and brought back Mariusa's father. Mariusa had been taken in the Ukraine when she was not yet even sixteen. Her father, who had somehow managed to find her address, had written her. After all sorts of formalities and petitions, Mariusa's father was exchanged for Kostya, one of our young fellows who didn't care where he lived. The meeting between the father and daughter touched us all; even the fat, dreaded "Wachman," Peter, who calmly beats up our lads for the smallest offense, was standing there with tears in his eyes. It's strange how in one person there can exist simultaneously such contradictory feelings as unlimited cruelty and sentimentality. Mariusa was embracing her father, running her hands across his face, and was covered with tears of joy. All the camp inmates surrounded them. It seemed that the atmosphere in our camp had changed completely. Everyone was happy, and they were singing songs the whole evening. No quarreling was heard, not even the shouts of the guards. I didn't even want to leave for Konkordia.

May 18, 1944   Today the kommandant informed me that Grewer would be leaving and I would have to be in the camp all the time. This is most unpleasant. Although our attic in the Konkordia could scarcely be called an apartment, nonetheless it has been more like one than in the camp, where there is no quiet. It is impossible to object. Yesterday a commission from Berlin arrived at the camp. This caused a great commotion among our girls. The previous evening they had all been told that everybody had to be dressed well and combed, and that the commission would check the intelligence level. The kommandant was supposed to select twenty girls. On the evening of the sixteenth, Olga, who worked in the kitchen, and Maria came running to me, all excited and in tears. They implored me to tell them the truth as to whether they were being taken to a bordello. I myself didn't know a thing. The kommandant was stubbornly silent, but nonetheless their suspicions seemed absurd to me, and I calmed them down as best I could. As a result, four did not appear at all, and of the sixteen who did, they selected eight for more specialized work at a military factory. Now there is a shortage of labor everywhere in Germany, especially since more and more people are being called into service.

June 16, 1944   On Sunday we went to Cologne. The impression is horrible: a mass of smashed buildings, mountains of rubble; it is simply impossible to ride down some streets. The picture is frightful. These are especially anxious times. Events are unfolding in the West. Since the beginning of June the English have been landing on the French coast. What will come of it? I only know one thing: that we have again fallen into the center of war activity, and we had thought that this would be a quiet and peaceful nook far removed from the war.

June 19, 1944   How have our girls gotten so pretentious? I simply cannot understand it. Tonya, who is expecting a child, got me very angry today. The kommandant had obtained a fantastic assortment of baby things for her: two blankets, sweaters, diapers, fluffy towels, and all sorts of things. I hadn't seen such charming items when I was expecting my children. A nice room in the new barracks had been set up for her and she was brought there from the crowded barracks where she had been living. On the very first evening she collected about a dozen girls in this room, and they even washed their hair there. This was in a room set aside for births! When I told her that this was absolutely impossible, she made a scene, went back to the barracks, and declared that she would give birth there. Painful as it is to realize it, one is forced to the conclusion that our people understand only when they are yelled at by the kommandant, as though they had become used to living under the whip.

June 20, 1944   Samanov received a letter from his friend from Leningrad. This fellow, who now lives in Karlsruhe, is happy that one can read so freely in Germany. "What a pleasure, this freedom of writing!" The Germans, however, feel that there is now a reign of terror among them. How relative everything is. Those who lived in Soviet Russia accept this terror as freedom. Our young people in the camp are very young and the majority are from the Ukraine, where life was easier, especially since their parents were taking care of them. But now they have to work hard far from home. Of course, many of them think of home as paradise. On top of this there is the fear of bombings and the constant air raid alerts. After the sleepless nights, they are not able to meet the work demands of the day. At times, however, they talk about the life of the German worker and then, especially the older ones among them, draw comparisons with Russia.

My Dima is head over heels in love with Paul's charming sister, Jeanne. Yesterday he accompanied her to the train, since she was going on vacation to the Munich area.

June 21, 1944   Tonya had a baby girl today. When labor began she moved very quickly into the delivery room. She had talked big when the birth was far distant, but now she was very happy to be able to lie down on a clean bed in a disinfected room. I quickly called the midwife and assisted her. Thus for the first time in my life I was present at a birth. I was greatly worried that I might do something wrong, or make an error in translation. The midwife spoke no Russian, and Tonya could not utter a word in German. Nevertheless, everything went very well. In two hours it was over. Tonya had conducted herself wonderfully and had not screamed even once.

July 1, 1944   A whole mass of shoes was delivered to the camp. I was happy that everybody would be able to receive some. But unfortunately this was not the case. Someone stole five pairs. The

Pretty and vivacious, Jeanne Ketter was one of the Luxemburgers who helped make tolerable those bleak days at the factory camp near Bendorf, Germany.

kommandant was enraged. He locked up all the shoes and declared that as a punishment there would be no distribution, and that the shoes would be sent back to Koblenz.

Grewer has been gone for ten days already. More and more workers are arriving. A charming girl named Valya arrived with the last transport. She is from Kharkov, a student and the daughter of a teacher. She was dressed very elegantly and is very attractive, but she gives the impression that she is quite fragile. Will she be able to do the heavy work which is required here?

July 12, 1944   Today I had to serve as translator for the the criminal police. Only this time it was really amusing. One of the French prisoners had been going with a young German girl from Bendorf for a long time. I had often seen them on the street and in the park. They had not even particularly tried to hide it, in spite of the fact that relations between German women and foreigners are now strictly watched. Recently a German girl in one Rhine town had her head shaved for too close a relationship with a Frenchman and was led through the entire town in shame. In the case of our Frenchman and the Bendorf girl, someone had apparently reported it to the police. I translated Roeder's questions and the Frenchman's answers. As a result Jacques, the Frenchman, got out of trouble, and Roeder declared that the German girl was also not guilty. However, the person who had reported this was accused of making a false report. (How happily we laughed when I met this girl, Anna, on the street about three months after the war. She had a charming baby in her arms, an exact copy of this Jacques.)

There is a noticeable tendency to treat the foreign workers better.

July 15, 1944   Today there was a scene with the kommandant. He has the disgusting habit of shouting when something is not done just as he wants it. I had scarcely entered the camp when he shouted at me in the presence of the "Wachmanyi" and some of the camp residents. I got angry and didn't say a word to him, not even when he had calmed down and addressed me. Then when he demanded an explanation from me, I very quietly answered him that if he would shout again, I simply would not come to work and I would let the director of Konkordia, whom I would inform, decide about our conflict. Thus I held out till the end of the working day, and at seven o'clock I went to Konkordia.

July 17, 1944   The kommandant is terrified that I might actually go to Director Wefelscheid with a complaint about him. It turns out that his coarseness is already well known to the administration, and the director was very much opposed to such treatment of the Eastern workers. Yesterday I purposely did not hurry to work, and arrived one hour late at the camp. Tanya was on time, and he had come to her several times to find out whether I was coming and where I was. Tanya had answered rather vaguely. When I finally arrived, he came to meet me, called me into his office, and even excused himself for his conduct. Apparently he is basically not a bad fellow, but just very crude, and that hurts him. Such a gentleman as Director Wefelscheid could not excuse the coarse outbursts of the kommandant. I accepted his excuses nicely, and with that the incident is closed, at least for the time being. I hope that now he will be more careful. This would be good both for me and for the camp inmates.

July 21, 1944   We are all shaken by the attempted assassination of Hitler. This will probably be reflected in Germany's entire policy and indirectly on us as well. Everywhere there is unbelievable excitement. All of our camp inmates are very disappointed that the attempt did not succeed, and they do not hide their attitude. This morning the kommandant went away somewhere.

July 27, 1944   One week has passed since the assassination attempt on Hitler. There has been no effect on life in the camp.

August 20, 1944   The camp kommandant has gone to the West, perhaps to the front, perhaps to the trenches. Everything is kept secret. Thirty Russians and two guards were transferred. Thus Peter, the greatest blight on my life, is gone. A certain Gueltz has come in place of the kommandant; this Gueltz is employed at a number of places simultaneously, and comes here only for a few hours.

August 30, 1944   A new director, Dr. Riess, has been appointed for Konkordia. He came to the camp, looked everything over, and spoke with everyone. I like him. He is pleasant in appearance, blond, about forty years old, apparently very intelligent and cordial. Our Eastern workers like him very much and expect a number of changes for the better. Yesterday he called Samanov and me to the plant in order to go through the shops together and to translate what he wanted to say to the foreign workers. The French and Italians, especially the latter, did not show any pleasure, since the production norms proposed by Riess were greater and, with the present food, would be difficult to fulfill. Our Russians, who had always managed to fulfill their norms, reacted favorably, asking only one thing, an increase in the bread ration. Indeed, in Russia bread is the main food of the worker, who will easily eat up to two kilos a day. If there would be enough bread, then the Russians would not be worried about the rest. I translated all of this to the director, and he promised to do everything he could. It is good that he is interested in the situation of the foreign workers, who comprise the main part of the labor force at Konkordia.

The day before yesterday there was a very nice concert in the camp. Musicians from Berlin played. This group bore the name "The Blue Duck." Before the beginning of the concert, there was a speaker. As in the Soviet Union, here, too, his speech was solid propaganda. In Soviet Russia they would have repeated the name of Stalin a hundred times; here the name of Hitler did not leave his lips. Our young people were silent, but they looked at each other and made hidden faces. At the end of the speech there was a little applause, most of it coming from the guards (who, by the way, had not understood a single word, the speech of course having been given in Russian). The concert and the skit were very good, and we all came to life.

September 4, 1944   Today is a wonderful fall day. It is already cool. Apparently the heat which had bothered us in August has ceased completely. How wonderful life could be if it were not for this war with its constant alarms and bombings which make everything so unbearable. From all appearances it seems that we are again near the front. Bendorf is full of military vehicles, just like two years ago in Pyatigorsk. The mood is tense and uneasy. I often go walking in the fields at night with the boys. Tanya, as before, is not interested and stays home. It does no good to try to talk her into taking a walk or get her interested. She told me that she doesn't want to live, and that it would be much better to die right away from a bomb.

Since we now often spend the night in the camp, I usually go to the bunker about a kilometer from here in the event of air raid alarms. It is in a cliff and was formerly a wine cellar. Hundreds of people gather there. Further on there are safer places marked out for the German population; the front ones, near the entrance, are for the foreigners. Who all is not represented there: French, Italian, Belgian, Dutch, our friends the Luxemburgers, and our entire Russo–Polish camp. We don't even hear the roar of the planes because of the conversations, and if it weren't for the fact that it was night and if we didn't have to work the next day, the time we spend in the bunker would be most happy. We have all become acquainted. The Italians look for pretty Russian girls, and soon there is flirting going on. Our boys are jealous and forbid the girls to speak with the Italians. But this is all rather peaceful, because we are all somehow united by the common danger and the situation we are in. I adore our Luxemburgers, and there is always something interesting to talk about with them. Among the French here, there are also many interesting, intelligent people. The time spent in the bunker flies past unnoticed, and when the all-clear sounds, we don't even want to go back to camp. Only the necessity of getting some sleep drives us back.

September 7, 1944   Today is a very dismal day. I am sitting in the camp all by myself. Gueltz scarcely ever comes any more; the young ones are at work; the night shift is sleeping; and only a few sick ones remain, along with one "Wachman"—Little Pete, as the Ostarbeiter call him. It is melancholy and the sky is overcast.

September 9, 1944   Yesterday I was in Koblenz. The city is in a real war situation. Every man has his documents checked. There are soldiers everywhere. The atmosphere is very tense. While I was there, there was an air raid alarm and I had to sit in the bunker two hours. It was cold and damp there. One consolation was that I was able to read an entire French novel, for which I had had no time in the camp.

Later that same day 2 o'clock in the afternoon   The sirens keep going continuously. Yuri is not with me and I am suffering. The anti-aircraft are firing all the time and huge fragments are flying around. I hope that Yuri has some common sense and is sitting inside somewhere. Nevertheless, it is horrible that since the age of five the child has been pretty much left to himself and has been constantly subjected to danger connected with the war. There are air raids day and night. There is no peace at all. I have just found out that bombs have been dropped on Neuwied; this is scarcely nine kilometers from us. One is afraid to go anywhere. But really, what difference does it make where you are when the bomb gets you? If you stay in one place it's all the same; you can't avoid your fate.

It is much calmer now in the camp without Reinhardt, the former kommandant. Only now do I understand what a pressure and uneasiness he caused with his constant shouting.

September 12, 1944   The Americans have simply gone crazy. They don't give us any peace at all. There are constant air raid alarms. It is impossible to undertake anything, since you spend almost the entire day, as well as the entire night, in the bunkers. Neuwied has suffered greatly, and today bombs were dropped on the Engers bridge. The explosion was very great. I had had to go to Konkordia on business, and the window panes there all shook and a few fell out. Tonight we shall spend the night in the camp, since everybody frightens us saying that Konkordia will be bombed, and our attic is right next to it and will fly apart like a house of cards from just one shake. Samanov spent all last night with us in the basement. It was very painful and sad, and he did not want to leave us alone. I feel simply terrible today; sleep is now much more important to me than food.

September 21, 1944   It is now three o'clock in the afternoon and the air raid alert has just ended. Today was the first attack on Bendorf, and an extremely heavy one. Both Bendorf and Koblenz, ten kilometers away, were bombed. A few bombs fell near the camp. One of them hit the house of our director, Wefelscheid. Everywhere they are putting out fires caused by incendiary bombs. All of our boys have been mobilized. When the alarm started we were in the camp, and when the bombs started falling we ran into the basement. The German women, the cook Maria, and Paula the seamstress, who has been hired to help Alexandra, were very excited. They haven't gotten used to this yet, and therefore treasure their lives more than our Ostarbeiter. Insofar as the latter are concerned, it was even difficult to drive them into the cellar. I persuaded our Vasya, a friend of Yuri's, and seventeen-year-old Kolya to come with us, telling them it would make it easier for us.

If the war continues, nothing will remain. Everything is being destroyed. The main thing is that for the most part they drop their bombs not on military targets but wherever they land, destroying hospitals, houses, and the civilian population. We cursed the Germans in Leningrad when they smashed the hospital on the Soviet Prospect, considering them savage barbarians. But now exactly the same thing is being repeated. There is simply no way to save yourself. There is one refuge, the cliffs. However, the entire population of the city and its surroundings cannot be put there. We all live only for the present day, expecting that any minute can be the last. Yuri Samanov just phoned. He had heard that bombs had fallen near the camp and was worried as to whether we had been hit. It's nice that someone is concerned about us. I treasure this relationship very much.

October 5, 1944   We have survived till the 5th of October. There are alarms the entire day almost every day, and almost every night. Life has become completely senseless because of them. The last few days haven't been especially bad, but bombs were dropped. They say that Koblenz has been hit again. What a pity. It was such a nice, charming city. I remember it with pleasure. Only recently it was so nice there. Now it's supposedly just a mass of ruins. How horrible war is! There is no peace. Is it possible that it will still continue for a long time? Indeed, we long for peace and quiet, so that we can sleep peacefully, so that the children can be healthy and secure; but this small desire is unattainable. I often dream that the war is over and we arrive in Leningrad. At first we don't go right home, but to friends, to find out what has happened to my husband, whether he is alive. And suddenly it turns out that everybody is alive and lives in the usual place.

What a joy it would be to see them after so many years! Will this dream be realized some day? Will we survive?

October 12, 1944   Dima came for a few days. He is very thin. The food he receives, without any of the extra privileges which we have here in Bendorf, is simply not enough for him. I am very worried about him. Two boys who were studying in the same school with him have become ill with tuberculosis. I would have liked for him to remain here, but he feels that it is better for him to finish his studies there. Indeed, they did not accept him into the gymnasium in Koblenz, but in a private school called "Arle." The instruction is not the best, and also it is very expensive. We supplied him with a lot of fruit; the cook gave him some meat, cheese, and butter. Our friends from Luxemburg gave him a whole envelope of food stamps. This is the work of an underground organization in Luxemburg, comprised of opponents of Hitlerite Germany. They supply their own exiles in Germany. Our dear Ketters, seeing what poor condition Dima was in, shared their stamps with him.

A few days ago the actor Bolkhovskoi arrived. He had wanted to entertain our Ostarbeiter and read to them. He was famous as an artistic reader both in Leningrad and in Pyatigorsk. We have a new camp kommandant, and for some reason he was afraid and declared that Bolkhovskoi must be either a provocateur or a Communist, and thus forbade the performance. It is good that our new director, Dr. Riess, is such an intelligent and nice fellow. I went to him and explained everything. He allowed the reading, after first giving our kommandant a dressing down. As a result, this kommandant, Klein, became angry with me, and there were some subsequent unpleasant moments. Today Dr. Riess is calling me in for some type of explanation. All of this is very unpleasant. Bolkhovskoi has left,

having brought some entertainment and joy into our monotonous life, and a lot of unnecessary extra problems.

October 16, 1944   Life is uneasy. The radio constantly broadcasts
about planes flying in various directions. There were alarms
from early morning, and there was also one at night. But this
time I didn't react at all. Maybe because we here in the camp are
somehow more at ease, in spite of the fact that if even one bomb
were to fall here there would not be a trace left. Nevertheless, I
think that the Konkordia is a much more attractive target for
the planes, and it is more likely that it will be bombed.

The Italians from the western camp are constantly coming
after our girls and arousing the jealousy of the boys. Yesterday
at the plant the Russians surrounded our pretty, lively Olga,
with whom a handsome Italian had fallen in love (she apparently had not been at all opposed to this), and poured tar on her
from head to toe. She was simply in despair. Her dress, stockings, shoes, and linen were just ruined. There was no way they
could be washed or cleaned. Her hair was stuck together, and it
was impossible to comb it; her entire face had turned into one
black mass. At the very moment when the other girls were
washing her hair, hands, and face with gasoline in the factory
washroom, the Italian burst in; threatening and gesticulating at
the same time, he kissed her dirty face and somehow managed
to calm her. Even today, the next day, Olga still cannot get
clean, and the clothes she was wearing had to be thrown away.
The boys are not satisfied with this and threaten that there are
still four others who will get it. The girls are afraid even to go to
the dining hall, which is only twenty steps from the barracks.
The administration is reacting to this all too lightly.

October 18, 1944   Today something occurred in our camp which has caused a tremendous shock. We are all so crushed by it that it seems as though the life has gone out of the camp. A few days ago the police seized one of our youths in the ruins of a bombed-out house. He had stolen a pair of shoes there. The boy was arrested, and he was sitting in the town jail where they usually put the Ostarbeiter for all types of thievery. Although we knew that the punishment for thievery during or immediately after a bombing was much more severe, we nonetheless had hoped that in view of his youth and his not knowing the German law he would be let go. However, it is clear that the Germans wished to make something of a show trial to set an example. The order was issued this morning to have all those men not working the early shift brought to a certain place in the forest. No one had the faintest idea of why they were being summoned there; it was thought that they were being called to do some type of extra work. The "Wachmanyi" brought the men in three brigades to the designated place; and there in a forest glade was our poor Vanya, hanging from a scaffold. Later, the criminal police called everybody together in the camp and said that if robbery during air attacks did not cease, then everybody could expect the same fate.

November 7, 1944   Yesterday evening was the worst air attack of them all. Even in Leningrad I had never had to endure such a raid. We were seated and just about to begin supper when Kommandant Klein came in and said that a full alarm had been given and planes were already attacking. Even our ever-calm seamstress Alexandra returned, worried, after she had gone out to the yard to look, and persuaded everyone to leave the hall. Yuri and I left the barracks. Outside it was as light as during the day. The guards were hurrying us into the cellar. This cellar was situated under the kitchen and the office and couldn't have saved anyone. If a bomb were to fall even on a neighboring barracks, everything would collapse and bury this famous "cellar." While we were walking the five steps that separated us from the cellar, we were blinded by a bright searchlight and deafened by a terrible crash coming from somewhere. Fragments were flying in all directions. All my self-control disappeared; I couldn't see the stairs, my legs were shaking. I was holding Yuri by the hand. People were running from all directions. At this moment somebody seized me by the arm and helped me down the steps. In the cellar he embraced me and calmed me down. I recognized Vasya. He was always there when danger threatened, always calm, and he would always leave with empty hands.* I asked him, "Where are your things?" Everybody had at least a small suitcase with him. He answered, "All the photographs are always with me. I made a special bag and carry it with me under my shirt." His treasures were the photographs he had taken from Russia.

We were standing in the cellar two hours, Yuri between Vasya and me, quiet as a mouse. Poor boy—how much he has had to endure. The building shook. Everything was clattering. We could hear the bombs exploding, the anti-aircraft firing. When everything had finally grown silent, we left the cellar. It was light on the streets, just as it had been two hours before. From the direction of Koblenz everything was in flames. Unceasing explosions were still audible there. Obviously a powder dump had been hit. This night we slept fully dressed. Yuri's cold became worse, of course. He is coughing and sneezing.

November 16, 1944   Two of our girls, Sasha and Katya, have got

---

*In his desire to help, Vasya would leave his own belongings behind. During the bombings people always took essentials with them in case they were bombed out.—Ed.

tuberculosis. This is very depressing. Both of them were very nice, especially Katya, who has a very bad case of TB. She breathes very heavily and almost never leaves bed. When you go to see her, you find her in tears; she is afraid of dying in a foreign land. In addition to being very sorry for these nice people, I am also afraid of Yuri catching TB. Indeed, you can't get him out of the barracks. He is friends with everyone and visits the sick ones. One of them, Sasha, had even been giving him Russian lessons at my request. He had always fooled around when I tried to teach him, but with her he was always diligent. It was only after he had been working with her several weeks that I discovered that she has an open form of TB. Now I am frightened out of my wits that Yuri might have been infected. And this fear is even stronger than that I have of the air attacks. For if one of the bombs falls on us, we'll die immediately, and all of us together.

November 23, 1944   I am writing much less often. The days are flying past so fast that one doesn't even have time to turn around. Camp life is monotonous; every day there are minor misunderstandings, problems, etc. For example, we were able to get thirteen women's coats. It was necessary to choose whom to give them to, since there are more than fifty girls here. It is very difficult to act fairly. They all want them, and some hide the fact that they already have one. As a result, as always, there are a lot of dissatisfied girls.

Recently I have become friends with the economic director of Bendorf, and he does quite a lot for us. Now he has promised us such rare items as stockings for the girls.

November 24, 1944   Today the newspaper carried an interesting manifesto by Vlassov.* It had tempting promises: there was to be private property, the abolition of the *kolkhoz*,† etc.

The alarms haven't ceased since early this morning. Planes have been flying uninterruptedly overhead, perhaps by the thousands. Apparently they have been bombing in the neighborhood of Koblenz. Even here the earth was trembling. Yesterday, in going through the city, I noticed a line for the first time; the people were standing by the bakery for bread. It was the same thing at the meat shop. Until now there had never been anything like this, even though the war is now in its sixth year. But only now that the country is surrounded and there are daily bombings are these shortages felt. How strange! But even now trains are running; you can go anywhere you want—all you need is to get permission from the police. All those who lost their belongings in the air raids receive various things from the stores. I am constantly amazed by this.

Kommandant Klein just came in and frightened us all with his announcement. He had returned from a consultation with the plant director. They had spoken about the fact that if the Anglo-Americans approached closely, we would have to burn all the papers, take a supply of bread, and all go on foot to Thuringia. Is it possible that we shall again have to move somewhere, and, moreover, under such conditions? Winter is approaching. It is already getting dark early and it is very cold, especially at night. In addition, we would have to leave all our things behind, and how far could we get on foot? Several people in the camp are very ill. What could we do with them? Question after question, and there are no answers.

---

*A Russian general who, when captured by the Germans, wanted to set up an anti-Stalin Russian government. Hitler, however, did not want the Russians to share in the victory. When the Germans finally let Vlassov recruit among the Soviet prisoners, it was too late to influence the war.—Ed.

†This is a collective farm.—Ed.

Valya had been a student before being sent to the factory camp near Bendorf. Elena Skrjabina feared that she was not strong enough to survive the rigors of camp life.

December 11, 1944   The ninth was Yuri's name day and he received a lot of money. He announced that he had already saved 130 marks toward a car, which he was going to buy after the war so that he could drive me around.

On Sunday there was a show in our camp put on by the residents themselves. Late in the afternoon there was a heavy bombing, but toward evening everything quieted down.

December 16, 1944   The Russian workers put on something resembling a strike. They stopped work because they were given some very bad soup today. Director Riess summoned me to go through the different shops and transmit his words to the workers. After negotiations, all of them again went to work, having obtained a promise of improvement of the food. As a result, Maria, the cook, has been relieved of her duties and Frau Moyre has been appointed to her place. The director had been informed that Maria had constantly been making special meals for her friend the "Wachman."

December 19, 1944   Yesterday while we were sitting in the basement of the Konkordia, because the air raid alert had come while we were at the plant, a German acquaintance entered and said, "Someone has come to see you." To my great joy I saw Dima. He looked terrible: thin, tired, and all muddy, since a few times en route from Koblenz he had had to lie down on the ground for protection against flying fragments. Nonetheless, he is with us now, having come to spend the holidays. I am trying to persuade him to stay here for good. What kind of learning can there be when you don't know what will happen to you from one minute to the next.

January 4, 1945   Our mood for this New Year is terrible. On the thirty-first there was an air raid on Bendorf. In the roughly five minutes of the raid more than half of the city was eliminated. There are many dead. For several days they have been digging out the dead and those buried in the ruins. Some of the latter are still alive. The city looks frightful. All these little houses collapsed like a house of cards. All the streets are buried in rubble, and people are moving about in them. The impression is depressing, crushing. All the foreigners, Russians, French, Belgians, and Italians, are helping dig out the dead. They are working without halt; the common catastrophe has united them. All the town inhabitants, numb from horror, have started to leave with their belongings for the woods, for Sayn, and the bunkers. They are all being gripped by a general panic. One doesn't know where to go. We have spent two days in the bunker, but it is cold and damp there, especially in the front part. Further in, it is so full of people that it's difficult to breathe. Now we no longer hide in the camp basement, since it will not save anyone from bombs. We run to the bunker at the first wail of the air raid siren. There are also frequent alarms at night; but for some reason they have now stopped bombing at night. The last nights have been peaceful.

January 6, 1945   A bomb has fallen on the house of our former director Wefelscheid. A great number of incendiary bombs have been dropped, the opposite shore of the Rhine is in flames, and there are many fires on our side. During the raid Yuri and I were in the bunker and didn't hear anything. Only we got very tired of standing on the ground. It was full of people and difficult to breathe. There was nothing to sit on. All the local inhabitants bring folding chairs and little benches with them. I have become so weak from these raids that I decided today to speak with the "personnel chief" of the factory. He dissuaded me from leaving. He said that there is still no real danger. Of course I realize that it is risky to go to Thuringia, but remaining here in such a time when you can expect any day to have a bomb land on your head is also not very joyful.

   Where in Germany can one find a place where there will be no bombs and where one can live peacefully?

January 9, 1945   Today a transport is leaving for Thuringia. We could have gone too. Again, as in Leningrad on August 23, 1941, I missed the last transport. Did I make the same mistake today that I made then? Today I received a letter from Varya, who has been living in Thuringia for more than a month and who is satisfied with her life there. She writes that everything is quiet. During all that time an American plane has flown over only once and dropped mines. That is of course the good side; but how many other questions then arise? The main question is that of food. Here we receive food prepared from the factory kitchen, or else we receive it in the camp. The ration issue of food by coupons has been reduced. Adults receive only 250 grams of butter a month. But in Thuringia it is probably no better. I can't imagine how we could make out on such rations. We know from experience what starvation means, and there is nothing worse! To have to endure this again is unimaginable!

Not only Martini, the chief of personnel, dissuades me, but also Dr. Riess, whose opinion I respect highly.

I have received a letter from my old friend Miltenberg. He invites me to come to his estate, assuring me that it is far better and quieter than on the Rhine.

January 11, 1945   We are now having a real Russian winter. The streets are covered with drifts. The trams are no longer running, and it's difficult to get through by bicycle. Yuri and I go everywhere on foot; sometimes we walk several kilometers. Our feet get very cold. I am very sorry I don't have my warm "valenki" (Russian felt boots), which Dima had sold for me in Kiev en route to Germany. They would indeed come in very useful now. It is true that the Germans would be astounded by such footwear; however, they themselves are in no way prepared for such cold. I have no boots, and galoshes don't keep one warm. It is very cold in the barracks in the morning; the walls are very thin. You can see outside through the cracks. The wind blows right through. I remember our solid Leningrad apartment.

Yesterday a fifteen-month-old girl died in the camp; she was the daughter of a Frenchman and a Polish woman. I feel very sorry for her parents; they are both crying. This girl had absolutely everything. Her parents had received packages from France. She was dressed like a doll. She also ate reasonably well. Her parents adored her and took wonderful care of her, and despite this, this sweet creature had to die.

January 12, 1945   Yesterday evening, just as I was getting ready to read, the lights went out. We had to sit in darkness the whole evening. Both of our seamstresses, Alexandra Ivanovna and Paula, the German woman, came and we talked. But unfortunately all of the conversations are either about camp gossip, which is already quite boring, or about war happenings. And since no one really knows anything definite, that is also gossip. Some say that everyone from the camp and even the inhabitants from Bendorf will be evacuated, and only the sick and those with children will remain.

The first transport was very small; only about 200 people were on it. According to eyewitnesses, this transport was very well fitted out, all second class cars and no change to Thuringia. Involuntarily I began to envy those who had gone and was sorry that I had not joined them.

The artillery fire does not cease. I believe that people who have not lived through this "entertainment" will have a difficult time understanding what twenty-four hours of continuous firing from long-range artillery is like. Sometimes it is so strong that the buildings tremble.

January 17, 1945   The alarms during the last days have become more frequent. There is no rest either night or day. Two days ago it continued till two o'clock in the morning, yesterday till midnight. We never really get a chance to sleep. We just doze off and are awakened by nightmares. We're listening all the time, afraid that we'll miss the siren. It's very difficult to run to the bunker, especially at night. The path is slippery, it's dark, you stumble and almost fall, you are panting from the quick walking up the hill and you begin to cough.

I am constantly afraid that Yuri's nerves will break. There has been no news from Dima since the beginning of January. Nothing came of my attempts to persuade him to remain here. He insisted that he must finish school.

I get almost no mail. Where is Dima? What is happening with him? I don't even know whether he made it back all right. Yesterday a bomb landed on the bridge across the Rhine at

Neuwied. Everything is being destroyed. Life is becoming a nightmare both in dreams and in reality.

And in the camp everything is taking its normal course. Three days ago one of the girls bore a daughter, a large healthy baby.

It's a pity that the Germans are in the hands of a semi-mad cretin just like Stalin. If it were not for this, this country would have gone far. And now wherever you look, everything is being erased from the face of the earth. It's a good thing that no one around here can understand what I am writing or is interested, or things would not go very well for me.

January 19, 1945   The siren awakened us at one thirty in the morning. Immediately after that a few bombs fell very close to the camp. We had to run to the bunker. Snow mixed with rain was falling. The bunker was very overcrowded. Now some people just remain there and don't leave it at all. They have even arranged real sleeping places for themselves.

January 24, 1945   Several letters finally arrived from Dima. He writes that he gets enough to eat, that he is studying and is satisfied with his situation. But now I am worried about Yuri. He always has a cold, but till now it was only a head cold. Now, however, it has gone deeper and he has a bad cough. He can't go to bed because any minute there can be an alarm and we'll have to run to the bunker. Today, it's true, we didn't even go anywhere; we simply sat at Alexandra Ivanovna's. I don't know which is worse, air attacks or illness. I myself have a bad cold, and apparently because of this I am quite apathetic today. I would just like to lie down and be left in peace by everyone. But that is just impossible.

Our Ostarbeiter came to complain that one of the foreman is

like a beast and hits them without any reason. They asked me to transmit that to the director.

January 26, 1945 I went to Dr. Riess yesterday to talk about the foreman. But this matter is far from over. He has done other things: stolen flour from a box car and boots and wood from a warehouse. All of this was covered up because of his connections, and maybe this too would have been kept quiet, but now it was reported. Yesterday they questioned all our boys and wrote down their testimony. It will be interesting to see what comes of this.

January 31, 1945 Today I saw Samanov. He is engaged to a German girl from Bad Ems. He is in excellent spirits, as though there were no war and no bombings. He and Dr. Riess get along very well, but all the other foremen and engineers are grumbling that he skipped out on the work of cleaning up the city of Bendorf after the bombings. Everybody from the simplest worker to the chief engineer is busy with that work now.

February 5, 1945 It's pouring rain. There is no snow. It's as though winter had already ended. Tomorrow will be exactly three years since we left Leningrad.

Today for a change I received several letters. One was from Consul Walter, who is now in Germany and is interested in how we are making out, and the other is from Colonel Schwartz, our friend from Krivoi Rog. He is still a patriot and believes in a German victory.

February 17, 1945 Spring is in full swing. It is warm and the sun is shining. They have already begun to prepare their vegetable gardens. There is no comparison whatsoever with the rotten weather of last year. I would like to spend all the time in the sun; however, the American planes prevent this.

Next to us in the barracks they are having a rehearsal of Gogol's *May Night*. The chorus of young voices is singing Ukrainian songs and drowning out the roar of the planes. These are flying in a long, steady stream in the direction of Frankfurt and Berlin, bringing death and destruction. This magnificent chorus of voices takes one far back, back to the white huts and cherry orchards of the Ukraine, and one wishes to forget, even for a little while, all the horrors of this terrible war.

March 6, 1945　All the older men have been mobilized into some sort of special detachments for defense against the Russians attacking from one direction and the Americans from the other. These units are called the "Volkssturm." At Konkordia there were only elderly workers left, since the younger ones had long since been called up.

March 12, 1945　Events have been unfolding with tremendous speed. The powerful attack of the Americans began a week ago, and today I am for all practical purposes unemployed. The camp has been evacuated and all papers in the office were burned; the terrified kommandant also burned all my books.

I have moved again to the attic. Among the Russians, only the sick ones and those having children were permitted to remain. Under the pretext of being ill, that remarkably pretty girl Valya also remained. Since she was afraid to stay in the camp alone, she, too, came to our place. As a child she had had polio, and this saved her now from having to go lord-knows-where and lord-knows-for-what. Later Polya and her friend Victor also came. They fled from the transport while it was moving.

The French translator told me that thirty French prisoners of war, who under no conditions wished to leave, were hiding out in a basement on the grounds of Konkordia. Nobody knew anything about this basement. Here they were safe, of course; however, they had very little to eat, and we have to help them somehow till the arrival of the Americans, which is expected any day now. I promised to think of something.

He had scarcely left when there was a knocking on the door. I was afraid that we had been reported and that we would be arrested, for on the attic floor next to our quarters there were two Frenchmen hiding out. However, it was only Dr. Riess. He asked Valya and me to go back to the camp and get the medicines which had been left there. We set off on our bicycles. It was a very eventful trip. Several times en route we had to jump off our bikes and throw ourselves to the ground, since there was almost uninterrupted shooting and shells, fragments, and splinters were flying all around. We returned safely, having gathered what we found.

In the camp there were still nine people with food for several days. They were not at all worried, since they were sure that the Americans were very near. Judging from the sound of the artillery firing, they were. Somebody from the local population had crossed over the Rhine and said that all the villages and towns on that side had already been occupied by the American forces.

In our attic apartment and the empty attic adjoining it, there are two more fugitive French hiding. During our absence Dr. Riess had dropped by again to find out whether we had returned. The entire doubled population of our attic was frightened to death, and hid wherever they could upon the sound of the footsteps on the stairs. Tanya, who opened the door for Dr. Riess, was nearly dying from fear that one of the stowaways might cough from the dust and then our entire conspiracy would be discovered. Fortunately nothing like that happened. Tanya promised him that we would go right over to him as soon as we returned, and he left.

March 13, 1945   The Americans are already in Neuwied. There has been uninterrupted firing the whole day. Valya and I obtained some food from the cook and, keeping part for ourselves, put the other half in a suitcase and went to the factory, having first obtained permission from Dr. Riess to go for some books which were in the factory library. This library was located right in the same building under which was the cellar where the French were. Everything went perfectly. One stood watch by the door while the other, after the straw-covered trap door had been raised, lowered the food into the eagerly outstretched hands. Right after this we quickly threw a couple of books into the suitcase and ran home.

The entire population of Bendorf has been ordered to leave. Frau Theby, the secretary of the director, also wants to leave on foot. Dr. Riess has been called into the Volkssturm. We have moved into the cellar where all the residents of our three-floor building sleep. We lowered two beds in there. Tanya and Valya sleep on one of them and Yuri and I on the other. Half frightened to death, Polya, Victor, and the two Frenchmen remain in the attic. They are no longer afraid that anyone will find them there, but they are quite worried about shells. And that depends only on fate.

March 14, 1945   Everything has remained unchanged. There has been firing from late in the evening till morning. In the afternoon we sit in the attic and go to sleep in the cellar. The weather is beautiful. Everything is getting green. The air is magnificent, and the heart is heavy. It is unnerving, not knowing when and how it will all end. The planes roar over constantly. But the population has quit hiding from them. Shells are gradually smashing Bendorf to pieces. Again my thoughts take me back to the not-distant past. How nice Brailov was two years ago, when we were all together and the war seemed far away; we had already forgotten about starvation and only now and then were troubled by thoughts of the cloudy future. Had it been worthwhile to spoil life with such thoughts?

March 25, 1945   Today at nine o'clock Bendorf was taken by the Americans. Our neighbors in the cellar woke us up at six, telling us that the Americans were very near and and that there was already firing in the streets. I went up again to the attic and saw through the windows that tanks were going along the road; others were coming down the hills from the direction of Sayn. Then I returned to the cellar to inform everybody about what I had seen. We began to wait for whatever might happen. A little while later soldiers in brown uniforms wearing round shiny helmets tore the door open.

The Americans had arrived.

INDEX OF NAMES

INDEX OF PLACES

INDEX OF NAMES

INDEX OF PLACES

Skarzysko Kamienna, 110
Stalingrad, 53, 54, 55

T

Thuringia, 174
Tuszyn, 116, 117, 128

V

Vinnitsa, 84, 111

W

Warsaw, 114

Z

Zaporozhye, 80
Zhmerinka, 90, 92

Scriabine, Helene.
   After Leningrad : from the Caucasus
to the Rhine, August 9, 1942-March
25, 1945 : a diary of survival during
World War II / by Elena Skrjabina ;
translated, edited, and with an
introd. by Norman Luxenburg. --
Carbondale : Southern Illinois
University Press, c1978.
   190 p. : ill. ; 22 cm.
   First pt. of this diary, previously
published in Russian, was combined
with a later account and published in
German in 1972 under title:
Leningrader Tagebuch.
   Includes index.

(Cont. on next card)